DUTCH DRAWINGS AND PRINTS

J. G. VAN GELDER

DUTCH DRAWINGS AND PRINTS

WITH 224 PLATES
IN PHOTOGRAVURE

THAMES AND HUDSON

LONDON

TABLE OF CONTENTS

Introduction 7

    I. Some Prints and Drawings from before 1500 9

    II. The Sixteenth Century 12

    III. The Seventeenth Century and Its Awakening 16

    IV. Rembrandt and His Pupils 19

    V. Rembrandt's Younger Contemporaries 23

    VI. The Eighteenth Century 27

    VII. The Nineteenth Century 31

    VIII. Vincent van Gogh 34

    IX. Symbolism, Realism, and the New Movement 36

        a. The Transition after 1890 36

        b. The Transition after 1900 37

Technical Data 40

Collections 43

Notes on the Reproductions 44

Short Bibliography 54

Sources of Photographs 54

INTRODUCTION

At no time, probably, have drawings failed to attract people's attention and arouse their admiration, although they have not always done so in the same way. Drawing has of old been regarded as a beginning: the first attempt to define ideas from which works of art in any media may grow and come into being; a way that may lead from drawing to print, from sketch to painting, from design to sculpture, building, or one of the many other creations possible to human hands. The work that we see in finished form only — a miniature, a portrait sketch, a composition in which care has been lavished on the smallest details — has almost always been preceded by a first rough sketch or at least a scribble.

The question arises whether we can justify grouping together and writing historical accounts of "drawn thoughts." We can assign them a place in the process whereby works of art are created. By themselves, however, they may seem hardly to belong to the realm of works of art. After all, is it not true that as spectators and users of houses or art objects we are only concerned with the end product? There is certainly much to be said for this point of view.

Many artists have expressed the wish that their drawings be destroyed after their death. Fortunately, such requests have not been carried out often; and we should be all the more grateful for this when we recall that original creations of artists of the stature of Michelangelo and Pieter Bruegel have been at stake. At the same time, we may speculate whether this is not why, except for the occasional sheet that chance appears to have preserved, we have practically no drawings by some of the greatest masters of the Low Countries, for example, Frans Hals, Vermeer, and Jan Steen. As against this, the abundance of drawings by other artists — the thousand and more drawings by Rembrandt or Van Gogh — also sets one thinking. The disparity in numbers, at times the complete absence of one characteristic example, makes it difficult for the art historian to present a balanced and responsible over-all picture.

Inasmuch as we limit ourselves in this book to drawings by painters and graphic artists, we are not too badly off as far as the Netherlands are concerned. The abundance of examples, even if they are somewhat unequally distributed, renders the task of making a general survey difficult, to be sure, though in no way impossible. The same profusion is unfortunately not to be met among sculptors' drawings, and still less among designs by architects. Alas, a general survey of the last two categories is not practicable for the Netherlands at the present time.

A survey of Dutch drawing of the last five centuries by no means amounts to a history of the visual arts during that period. For that history, more is needed than drawings alone. The characteristics of a given period can be brought out properly only if the total artistic production is taken into consideration. But, in that case, what sort of general picture can we get from drawings? It cannot be denied that, apart from all personal forms of expression, a general process of development and change can be traced in a chronologically ordered series of examples. Certain periods reveal particular characteristics precisely because of the way in which the art of drawing was developing at those times; and this cannot be entirely accidental. On the contrary, we shall see that even changes in drawing technique or preferences for specific media are inseparably bound up with a particular age and with the then current artistic styles.

There is still more to it than this. Drawings take us into the artist's workshop, and they also take us along whenever the artist, armed with a sketchbook and chalk, pen, or pencil, exchanges his studio for another place of work or for the open air. The history of the artist's expanding field of observation is the history of the visible world. This world, although different for every individual and for every artist, in every period calls for new methods of interpretation. Thus, we arrive at a history of the way in which man has recorded his experience.

Time and traditions pose problems and arouse longings. For the artist, the visible world has a twofold significance. It can be end and it can also be means, means toward the shaping of the images evoked by legend, story, belief, tradition, or history. The subject matter ranges from the simple yet mysterious story of our Saviour's birth to complicated reconstructions of historical events lying far in the past; from narratives out of the treasure chest of the human comedy to forms and visions of a world that has its existence in the dreams and thoughts of men. Alongside this the visible world is no less varied as a goal in itself for the spectator. It is infinitely rich in data. It is continually presenting a different aspect, because the spirit of every age is forever changing. The heart and eye never tire of singling out and perpetuating as motifs new aspects from the storehouse of visible phenomena that forever present themselves in new guises. It all lies in the choice made. In some instances it will happen that the motif (a tree, a nude, an animal) strikes one as an age-old refrain, but the way in which it is rendered is fresh and new. In other instances a totally new motif may turn up to startle us without bringing any change in the style of drawing. Normally, both subject and form are extensions of an existing repertoire and the illusion of a representation never previously conveyed is added as a creative element to mankind's endless series of visual concepts.

As soon as we begin to concern ourselves with drawings we are faced with many possibilities and expectations. The ever-changing history of how men have recorded what they have experienced or felt, conjectured or remembered, is intrinsically bound up with what artists working with pencil, pen, brush, or chalk have for centuries committed to paper or parchment, hesitatingly or confidently, passionately or deliberately.

I. SOME PRINTS AND DRAWINGS
FROM BEFORE 1500

It would be unrealistic to expect to find a distinctively Dutch style of drawing at a time when the area north of the Meuse, Waal, and Rhine rivers was still internally divided, even though the area formed the diocese of the Bishop of Utrecht (a prelate whose worldly interests were continually clashing with those of his neighbors). Not until the sixteenth century, when unity was initially achieved under the Spanish Hapsburgs, did a sense of Dutch nationality come into being. Soon afterward, the Protestant-inspired revolt against Spain led to the beginning of a lively, enterprising age for the new republic of the Seven United Provinces. Nevertheless, even in the loosely organized and relatively isolated delta area, something like a North Netherlands school managed to arise in the 14th and 15th centuries.

From time to time – now from the west, now from the south or east – cultural and artistic influences made their way in. They left some mark, it is true, on the art of the Low Countries, but the isolation and homely character of the region caused these influences to be brought to artistic expression in a peculiarly individual manner. We also hear of artists from the North Netherlands who left for foreign studios, seldom to return. However, those who did come back found signs of thriving artistic activity, especially in architecture, sculpture, and trade in works of art, in such important centers as Utrecht, Haarlem, and Delft. We know hardly any names of painters of before 1400 but we do have the names of some sculptors and miniaturists, especially at Utrecht, where examination of unfinished sections of miniature paintings shows the preliminary drawing to have been carefully prepared in a distinctive style. Such a study reveals that in the studios of the miniaturists working methods were quite different from those used in painting studios, such as those of Van Eyck and Rogier van der Weyden, where silverpoint drawings were used.

In any case, from the illuminated manuscripts that have come to light in and around Utrecht or at the Court of the Guelders Duchess Catherine of Cleves, we can see how, around 1430, animals and people were roughly indicated in small landscapes, how trees and foliage were still very sketchily done and followed an arbitrary scheme, and how figures and, somewhat later, interiors were represented with great exactness. Such interiors display a quiet, intimate character that one might fairly call Dutch.

It is no less striking how not only this character but also this manner of representation are found again in Dutch printmakers. The makers of woodcuts appear to have sprung from the ranks of the miniaturists and to have become the illustrators for the numerous books that began, after 1480, to appear in every intellectually flourishing town – Utrecht, Gouda, Haarlem, Delft, and Leiden, for example, and, after 1530, Amsterdam, which thereafter took the lead. The artistic level was not very high, it is true, but the work is quite lively. Outlines are broad and angular and the cast shadows are made up of short parallel lines. Trees and plants are themselves hardly more than outlines. But, after 1480, the artistic level rose; the political operations of the Dukes of Burgundy led to the establishment of closer relations with the more highly developed southern provinces, and the results of this development began to be felt.

Utrecht – chiefly important in connection with Late Gothic sculpture – became an influential center for miniature work, a field on which the accomplished Adriaan van Wesel (c. 1499) was to leave his mark. For painters' studios, however, one has to look to Haarlem (Ouwater, Geertgen tot Sint Jans) and Leiden (Huyg Jacobsz, the father of Lucas van Leyden, Cornelis Engelbrechtsz and his pupils); and also perhaps to Gouda and Delft. We also know of the artists known as the Delft Master and the Virgin Master without knowing where they lived, but no drawings by any of these painters have been pre-served. There is only one contemporary of theirs whose drawings we do have: the North Brabanter Hieronymus Bosch.

Let us first turn our attention to the copper engravers of about 1500. In contrast with the surrounding

I. Landscape with Rocks. Haarlem book illustration; 1485; woodcut; $7\frac{3}{4}'' \times 5\frac{3}{8}''$.*
Koninklijke Bibliotheek, The Hague

countries, where their number is fairly large and their work original, here we know the names of only two and their work is more or less imitative, based largely on paintings. In the twenty-six prints we possess by the Master I. A. M. of Zwolle — probably identifiable with the painter Johan van de Minnesten who became a guild member in 1462 — we find in a *Crucifixion* an affinity with, among others, Geertgen tot Sint Jans, and, in a rare, finely composed engraving in the Museum Boymans, *Madonna and Child with Cherries,* with Schongauer. The mother, engrossed in her reading, is flanked by St. Agnes and John the Evangelist; the alcove has been cut away, and one sees a landscape with ships and swans before the gate of heaven, with the meeting between Mary and Elizabeth in the foreground. The fine shading, the stippling, and the lively lines betray the goldsmith's schooling and the mastery of an engraver who, lacking, perhaps, the direct expressiveness of his contemporary Schongauer, amply compensates for this by a love of detail and a quiet intimacy. In the work of the Zwolle Master (Zwolle was a trading town situated on a river) we can see how elements from Westphalia, the Upper Rhine, and the North and South Netherlands were drawn together to be absorbed into a single style.

The second engraver is the architect Allaert du Hameel, born in 's-Hertogenbosch. He was municipal architect of Louvain (1495–1502) and was living in Antwerp in 1500, but he also took part in the completion of the St. Jan's cathedral in his native town. The twelve prints that we know to be his all mention the name of the town.

His prints of, for example, a monstrance, a Gothic canopy, and an ornament, show Du Hameel to have played an important role as architectonic decorator. His engraving *The Raising of the Brazen Serpent* has the merit of being an independent composition with a feeling for space and plasticity. The decorator is also recognizable, not only in the ornamental *entourage,* but also in the ingenious way in which the poisonous snakes are entwined about some of the figures. This is still a completely Gothic and unclassical solution that goes back, perhaps, to a piece of sculpture; but the way in which it has been worked out shows, especially in its solution of foreground problems, a wealth of imagination such as no Brabant sculptor had at his command. And if one has moments of doubt about the originality of vision possessed by these engravers, such doubt is impossible in the case of the great artist from 's-Hertogenbosch, their contemporary Hieronymus Bosch, who must certainly have had close contacts with Du Hameel, and who was, like Du Hameel, a member of the Onze Lieve Vrouwe Fraternity (for which the Utrecht sculptor Adriaen van Wesel was also working at the time).

Hieronymus Bosch is the first painter from the North Netherlands to whom we can ascribe drawings with any certainty. These differ strikingly, however, from the traditional, extremely careful silverpoint drawings with delicate lines, fine shading, and careful attention to detail such as are generally attributed to Van Eyck, Van der Weyden and Van der Goes. Bosch, too, certainly made similar, detailed drawings — Plate 3 shows a model for a group of statuary — but he also jotted down ideas that could be worked up later. He also made finished drawings on occasion, perhaps to be given as presents. The fact that Bosch did not use silverpoint on a prepared ground but drew directly on paper with a pen is something new for these northern countries, though in Italy at this time Leonardo was using the same technique. In some ways this technique carries on that used by the miniaturists in making their preparatory drawings; but Bosch improvises imaginatively as he draws, and, in the course of doing so, pays close attention to the minutest scenic and even biological details.

What a delightful landscape would present itself to our eyes if we could think away the fantastic tree-man from the *Allegory of Gluttony.* But Bosch does not allow us to do that: he cannot see the world free of such perverted growths and imaginative symbols, the significance of most of which is lost to us. In this drawing the owl and the half-moon forebode disaster for that heathenish and lascivious scene enacted behind the grisly head with its disk-like hat stuck full of pins and pitcher from which the ladder (symbol of copulation) ascends. This alarming monstrosity representing gluttony (Gula) also appears in a representation of hell (wing from *The Garden of Earthly Delights*).

By 1500 the world of Bosch's imagination is sharply split. He stands, a tormented soul, on the

11

threshold of the world that was presently to find, in the measurable realities of classical form, a solution that it gratefully accepted. Bosch alternates between serenity and visions of terror. He conjures up monstrous flies and nightmarish animals that could fittingly accompany the Antichrist; and even in a religious motif like *The Entombment of Christ*, the frightened face of Nicodemus under the fantastic headgear shows something of what is troubling him. And yet Bosch knows that Christ himself remains inviolable. To the medieval spectator and the Church this deeply religious conviction must have clearly represented the real source of Hieronymus's images. No nightmare could disturb that.

II. THE SIXTEENTH CENTURY

When Bosch died in 1516, a younger generation, influenced by Dürer's prints, had already shown itself receptive to the Renaissance motifs that were by now common property in Italy. Jan Gossaert traveled there in 1508. In 1518 Jan van Scorel also went to Italy, after first visiting Nuremberg. In Venice and Rome he became conversant with the Italians, especially with the work of Raphael. During the whole of the sixteenth and seventeenth centuries anyone who wanted to become a respected artist made his way to Italy. As a result of this, Dutch art — and indeed that of the whole of Europe — took on another aspect.

There are, however, between the old, medieval and the new, Renaissance art, transitional artists whose techniques are still rooted in the past but whose artistic language and interest in human beings bespeak the Renaissance man. To begin, there were Jacob Cornelisz and his younger contemporary, Lucas van Leyden. In the work of the former the Renaissance influence is limited to the tighter grouping of his woodcuts, in which it is easy to see that he had some knowledge of Dürer's Passion series.

Plate 6 shows some scenes from the Life of the Virgin by Jacob Cornelisz in which the woodcut technique has been determined by the style of Dutch incunabula, and the manner of shading and the graceful treatment of trees and hills have been taken over from Dürer. But it is especially its grand manner that makes Cornelisz' work so important. The angular stiffness of medieval woodcuts has been conquered; the expression is more lifelike and the detail more natural; his landscapes have a sense of space and perspective. This is also true of his pen drawings, which indicate his liberation from an over careful manner of drawing. As a woodcut maker, however, he has a simplicity of line and a command of composition of great value in handling the new style of painting circular panes of glass.

While Jacob Cornelisz (c. 1475) was working in the up-and-coming city of Amsterdam, Lucas (c. 1489) was living in the thriving drapery town of Leiden. He was an infant prodigy: in his work there is hardly any traceable influence either of his painter father or of his teacher Cornelis Engelbrechtsz; and by 1508 he was already an engraver of some importance. In his *Raising of Lazarus* he managed to retain the tension in his grooved parallel lines yet succeeded better than Jacob Cornelisz in arranging his figures so that their emotions can be read easily.

In his *Ecce Homo* of 1510 his initial difficulties in drawing foreshortened faces have been overcome. The gesticulating group in the foreground grips the spectators' attention even more than the Christ group, which suggests a recollection of a *tableau-vivant* in Easter Week. Lucas is a keen observer of daily life; like Dürer he also made small genre pieces on non-Biblical themes such as milkmaids, toothpullers, and trumpeters. Among these, one of the best is an etching of Uilenspiegel's family (1520). He also drew from the nude and took suggestions for details from a medieval poetical work by Dirck Potter, *Der Minnen Loop* (a moralizing *Ars Amatoria*). His ornamental prints with typical Italianate symmetrically divided candelabra motifs became the basis for a new art of decoration that spread through Holland quickly. Lucas had always been sympathetic toward new ideas, and, after meeting Dürer in Antwerp in 1521 and a little later coming into contact with Jan Gossaert, he, too, began to choose subjects from antiquity. At the same time, as can be easily seen in his elegant engraving, *The Joys of*

II. Cornelis Anthonisz, The Devil of Cards and Wine. Woodcut; $10\frac{5}{16}'' \times 7\frac{1}{2}''$.
Rijksprentenkabinet, Amsterdam

this World and Mary Magdalene (1519), he rejoiced in the gay things of life. One has only to look at the delightful way in which he suggests the excitement of a hunting party in the open landscape. In spite of this, his figures still have something Gothic and mannered about them. For example, one can see the S-form in a sketch of a female saint. But it is quite otherwise in his signed portraits; some of them, from 1521, were probably done in Antwerp and display the same penetrating gaze we find in Dürer portraits. These are the people of the new world surging into being. In their use of shading they remind us of the engraver rather than of the painter. Yet the fact remains that Lucas did not always achieve in his paintings what he achieved in his prints.

Jan van Scorel, a slightly younger man, is a full-fledged painter. After his visit to Venice (1520–21), where he was influenced by the work of Bellini and Palma Vecchio, his apprentice days under Jacob Cornelisz were quickly forgotten. In Rome, under the protection of Pope Adrian VI, he enriched his powers of composition by becoming acquainted with the art of Raphael and Michelangelo. We know of no portraits by him but we do have sketches of compositions and motifs for landscapes, the former indicated with a few pen lines supplemented by washes to reproduce the effects of light and shadow, the latter containing accurately sketched clumps of rocks and groups of houses. These he developed into fascinating backgrounds for his paintings.

Maerten van Heemskerck, who was Scorel's pupil in Haarlem (1528), later produced, as a result of a few years' stay in Rome (from 1532), the two earliest and greatest books of travel sketches by a Dutchman. His great series of drawings, partly with the pen, partly with red chalk, enriched by a genuine feeling for plastic form, provides a basis for our present knowledge of the topography of Rome in the first half of the sixteenth century. His skill is incredible and his vision of picturesque Rome unique; especially surprising is his view of St. Peter's, then still in the course of construction. His drawings, because of their fine cross hatching, remind us of Lucas van Leyden's. His later drawings (after 1560) with their Old and New Testament illustrations, allegories, and representations of historical incidents, are entirely in this manner. They were intended to be printed; and this was done by Coornhert, the teacher of the distinguished Haarlem artist Goltzius.

Although this graphic tradition persisted for a long time, in the long run the influence of painting made itself felt more and more on the art of drawing. Red and black chalk and tinted papers began to be used, to give contrasting effects that weakened the importance of line. Lucas's pupils moved in this direction, substituting movement and a new color scheme for the language of line. Intermediate tones began to be used; the colored wood carving (chiaroscuro print) made its appearance among prints. Moreover, new artistic theories were making their way to the fore. The artist as inventor must have read widely; the spectator needed a high degree of intelligence to read the Biblical and, especially, allegorical incidents.

One of the most important wood engravers was Cornelis Anthonisz from Amsterdam, who simplified the complicated technique, restoring importance to outline. His picture content, on the other hand, is literary and cerebral, weakening the attention paid to nature. What is more characteristic of the new age, however, is the way horizons had been broadened by the new ideas, how each voyage of discovery added to men's picture of the world. But this also brought in its train new economic and intellectual tensions. More was attempted; more was dared. This was also true of art. Altarpieces increased in size; designs for carpets and for glass required more than life-sized cartoons.* The volume of orders forced artists to work faster; invention came before careful execution where drawing style was concerned. The art of indicating with a few lines now became a method of demonstrating ingenuity.

The numerous followers of Frans Floris of Antwerp spread this manner of drawing rapidly. Antwerp, in fact, was the teaching center. Pieter Aertsz returned from there to Amsterdam; Dirck and Wouter

---

* Accurately scoled preliminary drawings.

Crabeth, the great painters on glass, brought Antwerp's taste to Leiden, The Hague and Amsterdam. Their spirit and vivacity may still be admired in the famous windows of Gouda, and in their cartoons that have been preserved. Robust forms, preferably in antique surroundings, were to determine the nature of Dutch art in the sixteenth century.

Small models of the great windows were supplied to the persons who had commissioned them. Some of Crabeth's and Pieter Aertsz's models have been preserved; one of the latter's, his *Adoration of the Shepherds*, is illustrated here. For details they worked from studies. A portrait of a man illustrates how Dirck Crabeth saw his models. The chalk drawing has been touched up with the pen here and there in order to heighten its plasticity and help the glazier. The portrait makes one think of Venetian portraits and, indeed, of Venice itself. Dirck Barendsz of Amsterdam, another well known painter of the time, was for five or six years a pupil of Titian. He returned to Amsterdam in 1562. His large drawing, the *Venetian Ball* of 1574, shows him to have come under the spell of Titian and perhaps even more of Veronese. The plasticity of the most often printed of his drawings has been heightened by the use of body color and intermediate tones. The same influences can be seen in the work of his contemporaries, Cornelis Ketel — see his *Corporation Piece* — and Anthonie van Blokland, although these two artists may have been influenced earlier during their stay in Paris, where the Italians were enjoying great success. Illusionist effects, such as the framing of a composition by figures seen from behind, or invisible staircases climbed by persons in the foreground, were borrowed from foreign models.

The Reformation brought great changes. No longer were there orders for religious themes, and, instead, we find painters choosing allegorical or mythological subjects. Commissions for portraits and even family groups and civic-guard banquets became increasingly popular after Amsterdam, in 1698, joined the side of the Prince of Orange against the Spaniards. Although artists continued to visit Italy, the tendency toward internationalism was paralleled by a steadily increasing nationalism. The current of nationalism encouraged the tradition of portraiture; other typically Dutch genres, such as the still life, especially flower painting, developed separately. Landscape painting, which had hardly existed in the sixteenth century, became a favorite, drawing inspiration from the Flemish style of Pieter Bruegel. Indeed, many of the Flemish artists had fled north to the Netherlands, especially after the fall of Antwerp in 1585,

The most progressive group of painters was formed in Haarlem under the leadership of the young Hendrick Goltzius, an enormously gifted engraver in both copper and wood. He was also a draftsman and, after 1600, a painter of great versatility. But the other members of his group and many of his pupils were in many ways scarcely less gifted.

As an engraver Goltzius was influenced by foreign models, especially by Bartholemus Spranger; he also had a complete mastery of Dürer's technique — see his *Christ Borne from the Tomb by Angels*. In 1590–91, a journey to Italy brought him into contact with his great contemporaries. Plate 21 shows his psychologically clever portrait of *Giovanni da Bologna*. Italy also inspired him to turn his hand to landscape drawing and the study of nature: following the example of Dürer, he drew animals, insects, plants, and trees. In these drawings the poetic element that had been more or less absent in the sixteenth century again came to the fore, for example, in studies of trees and woods. In a mythological subject, too, the variation of three colors brings such a picturesque quality to his work that there can be no doubt about the importance of the poetic element. Besides the perception of real things, the impression made on artists by the new translation of Vergil's Georgics can also be traced here. Goltzius had become acquainted with this modern feeling in Italy from, among others, Caracci, Barocci, and Muziano, and he had learned there how much richer the appearance and mood of a work could become through the use of varied colors.

By the end of the sixteenth century, therefore, many traces of the new sentiments are to be found. *Natura Artis Magistra* is no longer an idle saying.

III. THE SEVENTEENTH CENTURY
AND ITS AWAKENING

Throughout the seventeenth century people were to see the landscape as an idyll, just as they had come to enjoy pastoral plays. The landscapes printed after 1615 emphasize the amiable side of nature; their details have been developed to convey a romantic effect. The improved political and economic situation, bringing with it a sense of satisfaction and security, had something to do with this, and the effects of the strong influx of exiled Flemish artists certainly ought not to be underestimated. It was particularly the younger men, those who could contemplate their new surroundings with open minds, who encouraged the new spirit.

If we turn back for a moment to the way landscapes were represented at the beginning of the century, we can see that Goltzius' study of trees was not an isolated phenomenon. His pupil De Gheyn, his contemporary in Utrecht, Bloemaert, and Bloemaert's fellow-citizen, Roeland Saverij, all seized hold of this theme. It was especially Saverij, who had worked for a long time in Prague and who knew the loneliness of the Bohemian woods, who, in Holland, succeeded in rendering human melancholy in terms of twisted roots and knobby tree trunks. He anticipates, in fact, such widely separate figures as Jacob van Ruisdael and Vincent van Gogh. De Gheyn, Bloemaert, and Saverij, about the year 1603, freed the landscape drawing from a linear, mannered rhythm. They discovered the value of straight-forward representation, enhanced by soft-colored tints. Plant, flower, and animal studies began to appear, especially in Haarlem, Leiden, and Utrecht. The desire to represent the visible world in all its aspects received encouragement: De Gheyn, for example, in his clever miniatures of insects and other animals, was encouraged by the botanist Clusius. This way of looking at nature was partly borrowed from Breughel's drawings, in which the artist tried to capture atmospheric brilliance by the use of fine stippling. We find it also in the work of Goltzius, and, later on, in the work of Claes Jansz Visscher and Buytewegh.

In addition to having this topographic interest, artists were beginning to turn their attention to farmers, fishermen and skaters. Picturesque incidents were sought out and found.

If one glances through the profusion of drawings that appeared in the seventeenth century, it is possible to trace, through all the diversity, certain features that existed in common. Italy improved many a weak talent. There was an increasing urge to travel, not only to Italy but also up the Rhine to Switzerland. Contact with the Flemish diminished, despite the fact that Van Dyck, and, even more, Jordaens, continued to receive numerous commissions. But the interest of those who traveled was now focused less on foreign art than on nature and the way people lived.

Although the works of Claude Lorrain and Poussin, Reni and Guercino, Velasquez and Zurbaràn, were not unknown in the Netherlands, their influence was small. If people went to look at works of art, it was the work of Titian and Veronese, of Raphael, Dürer, and Holbein that they liked; in court circles Van Dyck was popular. Nevertheless, the Dutch artist retained his individuality; it is this independence that forms the main strength of Dutch art. Even the Dutch artists in Rome, the so-called Bentveugels (birds of a feather) had their own way of looking at their world; so did the smaller group in France. The Italians held it against them that they only saw the outside of things; the French, that they put unimportant realistic details above the harmony of an exalted, classically idealized world. What the Dutchmen brought with them from the south was the memory of fierce sunlight; and the capture of the play between light and dark by means of a single line became an essential feature of their work. Caravaggio, who died in 1609, had numerous Dutch pupils, but they were mostly the less influential artists of Utrecht, who attempted to translate his realistic, dramatic pictures into candlelit scenes or charming pastorals. We possess few of their drawings, but a light brown pen-and-wash drawing, *The Four Elements*, by Gerard van Honthorst illustrates how, in the period from about

III. Werner van den Valckert, Plato. 1620; woodcut; $11\frac{13}{16}'' \times 7\frac{1}{2}''$.
Rijksprentenkabinet, Amsterdam

1620 to 1625, the artist sacrificed form and truthful representation to achieve the effect of light coming from a hidden source.

Another Dutch artist worthy of note was Gerard Terborgh the Elder, of Zwolle. He arrived in Italy shortly before Honthorst. Terborgh sketched picturesque corners and landscapes in the manner of Paulus Brill and Jan Breughel.

Such fine observation of detail is also apparent in the work of the painter from Kampen, Hendrick Averkamp. Averkamp tried by the use of delicate, somewhat variegated colors, to reproduce atmospheric brilliance, especially in his winter scenes. Less lively than some Flemish examples, his figures are often thoughtful despite the anecdotal way in which they have been observed.

At this time a great deal of importance was still attached to line, especially in portraits, engravings, and etchings, which were still as a rule reproduced by engraving technique, but the charm of the landscape prints of Esaias van de Velde and Buytewegh leaves this graphic element more or less out of account. When it comes to representing people, too, this technique is capable of graceful effects. If one compares Buytewegh's *Cavalier* with the heavier, but more effectively typified *Cavalier* by Frans Hals, it is Buytewegh who has remembered Goltzius' teaching and Hals who, with a painter's skill, strikes out a fully developed characterization with just a few lines. The same difference between the older and the younger mentality can be seen in Van Ravesteyn's extremely carefully planned drawing *Civic Guard of the Company of St. Sebastian* as against the sketch by Thomas de Keyser, who needed only a few lines, making the necessary corrections and intensifying the lighting effects as he painted. One can wonder whether these changes should be regarded as reactions to academic and humanistic ideas or as a result of the refreshing discovery that spontaneous everyday life outweighs mythology and the historical tale. Both answers are possible, but the second is certainly the more probable. By the time that Rembrandt had unmistakably appeared on the scene, every drawing technique and every theme had had its turn. And yet, despite the domination of realism, there was no sudden loss of interest in allegories, emblems, and religious and historical subjects. These themes were to be found again in Rembrandt, but he was to give them a decidedly new form, and often a new interpretation.

While there is no seventeenth century draftsman (apart from the Bible illustrator Jan Luyken, who lived late in the century) to whom we can assign more than 400 or 500 drawings, there are almost 1500 by Rembrandt and almost as many by his pupils, if we take them all together. It is as if the whole range of subjects has been transposed by these artists into Rembrandt's style.

Before we discuss Rembrandt and his school, there is still one artist we must deal with, even though only two drawings and fewer than twenty paintings can be ascribed to him. He is Hercules Seghers, and he occupies a special position as an etcher. Although a contemporary of the Van de Veldes and Buytewegh, he is no simple realist but a poetic creator of imagined landscapes. Using an extremely complicated technique he created about 60 etchings, including 12 of ruins; the 150 prints of these are all different, either through their different colored backgrounds or through the use of different inks, with which he experimented. He knew the romantic etchings of sixteenth-century engravers from the Danube area and was an admirer of prints by Elsheimer. He also imitated Italianate artists like Willem van Nieuwland. But this was all completely transformed into the marvellously personal renderings of an imaginative and melancholy dreamer. His etching of *The Great Tree*, in dark green enlivened by small white highlights, becomes a mysterious composition filled with indefinable vegetation and strange habitations. Another etching, *Rocky Landscape with Four Trees*, creates a prehistoric effect, and his *Books*, printed on gray prepared linen, have a mysterious air. He lifts his subjects out of the reach of time. This independent manner of seeing things, with its breaking away from tradition, is to be met in other artists too after 1625 — the start of Rembrandt's career. By way of illustrating this, Plate 55 shows a detached and medievally observed *Market Place* of 1629 by Pieter Saenredam and Plate 54 the same market place as seen by Gerard Terborgh the Younger a few years later. The latter is much more picturesque and, based as it is more on personal impressions, realizes more dramatically the bustle of the market. The total picture has won out over the details that went into it.

In summarizing what has been discussed up to now, it becomes evident that it is difficult to talk of a Haarlem, Amsterdam, Utrecht, or Leiden school. There are differences in drawing style: silverpoint sketches are found alongside delicately shaded and contoured pen drawings and wash drawings with few lines and strong light contrasts. In colored drawints the quest is for atmosphere. Many artists employed chalk more as a means of suggesting than of clarifying. For many of them a quick sketch was enough. Woodcuts disappeared, and copper engravings were to an ever increasing extent replaced by etchings. People were trying to free themselves from the restrictions placed on them by the technique of engraving and were attempting to capture the picturesque by the use of varying amounts of etching acid.

As far as subjects were concerned, the visible world served as model. In landscapes, the search was for picturesque motifs, vistas and atmospheric conditions. In portraits, the emphasis was on character, the way people looked in their settings. There was a desire for unity and coherence; and this led often to the sacrificing of colorful nuances to a modulated monochromatic tonality in which everything was dissolved. One sees this chiefly in painted still lifes, portraits, and landscapes. Historical and genre paintings retained their colorfulness the longest. In brush drawings the urge toward monochrome and the feeling for finely graded color predominated over the feeling for strokes of the brush. Academic drawing from the nude took on the character of an intimate event.

Meanwhile people continued to travel and the number of collected landscape impressions grew. But in their own country, too, Dutch artists were searching after picturesque genre pictures, after the intimate life of humanity. This is also true of animal paintings. In short, wherever possible artists were capturing life and trying to give to the momentary and passing a permanent reality.

IV. REMBRANDT AND HIS PUPILS

For Rembrandt the drawing was always the natural means of expression; more than any other it lent itself to the representation of the "history" that Rembrandt wanted to depict from religion or mythology. This predilection was not entirely a result of his education at the Latin school, nor of his training under Pieter Lastman, who had received his artistic education in Italy. Rembrandt needed a story because he found the emotional element in all human experience fascinating. The manner in which this emotional element shaped his style of drawing can be seen both in his earliest and in his last, extremely simplified drawings. He used, consequently, all the techniques we have mentioned, even silverpoint.

Rembrandt remained a painter, however; probably, drawing was not strictly necessary to his painting. But he had the art of quickly and accurately setting down the content of his imagination with a few lines and brushstrokes – and he enjoyed doing it. By leaving much out, sometimes by stating nothing at all, he succeeds in endowing a mere scratch, or a dot, or a single shade with tremendous significance. His imagination seeks out meetings between Biblical or historical characters; he then carries the story on, endowing it with the fruits of his own thoughts and conflicts. He involves himself in everything, including the everyday world, which had never before been rendered so completely in pictorial form.

The really striking thing is that every picture – however familiar it seems to us now – wasthen an original discovery, a realization on paper for the first time. Again and again it is a significant meeting whose story he retells: *Abraham and the Angel, David and Jonathan, The Return of the Prodigal Son, Christ with the Apostles*, and *Christ at Emmaus*.

He did not travel much – he never went outside the provinces of Holland and Utrecht – but he walked a great deal in the country around Amsterdam, and there, along the Amstel and in the villages, he found ordinary and yet new subjects for drawings and etchings. Despite the singular character of his style of drawing, his baroque manner does not stand alone. Rubens, Van Dyck, and Brouwer provide, in their different ways, further examples of the same style, as do some Italians — such earlier men as Veronese and Palma Giovane, for example, and contemporaries like Guercino. Elsheimer, admired by both Rubens and Rembrandt, also created landscapes and compositions in this way, with penstrokes and brushstrokes running through one another. But Rembrandt, in his tempo and his accent, is something different again, and excels all others.

Renaissance pictures were balanced about a central line. Mannerism brought with it the elegance of the curved line and the contrasting movement along the diagonals. The baroque keeps these but breaks the lines, envelops some parts in darkness, floods others with light. It lets the spectator guess and, in so doing, share the feelings of the artist, who brings him to this attitude by means of his special approach. Rembrandt exploited to the full all the possibilities of the baroque. Moved as he was by the visible world and affected by this inner emotion he summoned up a world that appeals to an emotion by which he interpreted eternal feelings in his own individual manner. Meanwhile, there can be traced in his work the laborious rise of the personal to the broadly human, to a "wise joy proceeding from his victory over human sorrow" (Schmidt Degener).

In his drawings it is unnecessary to distinguish the Leiden period from the Amsterdam period. After an unpromising start, with a strong emphasis on linear and Caravaggiesque contrasts, the level of his work rose about 1627/28 and an unbroken stream of drawings began. He first chose as subjects mendicant types and studies of heads; he drew himself and members of his family; he prepared religious themes. He made use of pen and red chalk; his drawings usually have a brown-and-gray wash, sometimes heightened with body color. One of the most striking examples of the first series is a portrait of Rembrandt's father which, partly in its use of various sorts of chalk, brush and body-color, shows how complicated Rembrandt's working methods were from the very beginning. For rendering the expressiveness and plasticity of his figures he cannot do without the help of surfaces of brushwork. This can clearly be seen in an early self-portrait and in the moving picture of his mother. The abruptly broken-off lines force the spectator to supply for himself what is missing and to experience the artist's emotion. Moreover, once Rembrandt had found a conception he was never completely finished with it; he was continually returning to subjects and treating them again.

When the inventory was made of Rembrandt's estate in 1656 the drawings appeared to have been arranged according to subjects; there were no fewer than twenty-five sketchbooks and full portfolios. One of these portfolios contained many enchanting sketches of Saskia's daily life and household activities, a masterly series to which later were added the reed-pen studies and brush drawings of Titus, Geertje Dircks, the nurse, and Hendrickje Stoffels, the companion of his later years. They recall the work of Chinese artists with their continual practice with the brush. After 1630/35 the number of narrative pictures increases. The sufferings of Christ, in particular, and the stories of Abraham, Joseph and David appear frequently. A picture of the *Carrying of the Cross*, c. 1635, lets us see the emotion with which Rembrandt handled the pen; it makes one think of Brouwer's style of draftsmanship. By 1640 he has become simpler, especially in the numerous narrative sketches, recognizable despite repeated corrections; his conception of space is becoming more comprehensive. The over ecstatic gestures gave way to expressions of despair or self-pity. Most of his pupils, although they interpreted his aims understandingly, lacked their master's ability to create a dramatic picture. Nor did they succeed in creating such an original composition as *The Prodigal Son* with such an absence of theatricality and with such expressive restraint. It may be that this skill derived from the many drawings Rembrandt had done in the open air. His delightful series of landscapes would — if arranged chronologically — form one of the most beautiful albums ever made of Holland. He has a unique vision and understanding of the essential elements, with the result that trees, houses, farms, roads, rivers and canals, all growing things and all man-made things become a unified whole in the all-embracing play of light and shade. In addition to the landscapes, which include views of Muiderberg, Amersfoort and Rhenen, as well as of Amsterdam – and even of London, after pictures by other artists – Rembrandt made many animal studies of dogs and lions, a dromedary, a young bear, elephants, horses and birds. We have chosen the powerful chalk and wash drawing of a *Lioness Devouring a Bird*. (We find her again, looking a little less impressive, in the allegory, *The Unity of the Land*, Museum Boymans.) The exotic element – welcome for enriching old historical tales – Rembrandt found in copying, or to put it more accurately, transposing twenty-odd Persian miniatures into his own drawing style and technique. Rembrandt, like other great artists, copied a good deal from others (among them Leonardo, Carpaccio (?), Mantegna, Tempesta). His *Homer Reciting Poetry* (1652), dedicated to Jan Six, recalls Raphael's *Parnassus*. Indeed, he possessed prints of Raphael's compositions and of those by many other artists. In many of his "borrowings," however, it is plain to see that the motif has been observed and composed in a completely fresh manner.

After the middle of the century, his compositions became less dynamic and more static with more compact shapes increasingly built up of a few scratches and outlines by the use of reed pen and brush. His technique became a sort of drawing by painting, unusually pictorial through its feeling for form and color. The vigorous portrait sketches in particular – see the one that has been called *Jan Six* – suggest the warm glow of his sparkling late paintings; they are intensely human, almost superhuman. In his later years he suffuses the surroundings of his sketches with light through the use of darker gradations of tone. *Christ Raising Jairus's Daughter* may serve as an example of this. It is a composition in which the lines accompany the gestures and which, in certain essential respects, permeate rather than define curtains, bed and intent bystanders; not line but light is the element that builds up space. What he achieves in his drawings he also succeeds in doing in his etchings. To achieve this he evolves an extremely complicated technique; etchings demand more care than drawings. Chronologically, the same development can be seen: the detailed account becomes more and more a summary of the deeply experienced essence.

Among the earlier etchings belongs the *Annunciation to the Shepherds*, a rich account that loses itself in the landscape and in details. The *"Six" Bridge* of about ten years later (1645) is already completely free of irrelevant decoration; the tree at the left is at the same time the light and the wind that plays through it; two lines at the right convey the lowering of a sail. Still more forcefully expressed are the branches on the right of the etching of *The Hunter* (1653). They are no more than a scribble and yet one can recognize the birds preening themselves there; below and to the left, another scribble: ducks. A few outlines: one can see mountains with domed buildings and a little village lying in front. Over and over again one finds imagination and life, which together become an unexpected reality.

Rembrandt's *Hundred Guilder Print* should be dated somewhere nearer 1645 than, as is usually done, 1650. Studies for it, such as for the camel on the right, date from c. 1640 and earlier. This magnificent print, which displays as compact an organization as the *Night Watch*, illustrates Matthew 19 in its great diversity; and in it Rembrandt speaks with his whole being.

Who in Holland could match Rembrandt? A look at his etching *The Three Crosses* will provide a clear answer: the wonderfully organized light effects confer on the ominous and irrevocable quality of this drama the somber power of fate itself.

His nudes form another chapter in themselves; they are people observed with a clinical eye. Is this connected perhaps with the fact that many of Rembrandt's friends were doctors? The portrait he made of one of them, Dr. Arnold Tholinx, surpasses all other portraits in the gentle humanity that radiates from it.

There are more than 180 etchings by his hand, many of them existing in more than one state; it is probable that there are at least 3000 printed by Rembrandt himself. For Rembrandt his etchings were not a sideline or a form of relaxation but an important part of his life's work; they are his deeply felt experience of life, communicated through a laboriously developed technique which enabled him by means of little to say much, and even more to communicate intense feeling.

IV. Jan Lievens, Border of the Wood. Woodcut; $8\frac{15}{16}'' \times 5\frac{11}{16}''$.*

Rijksprentenkabinet, Amsterdam

In the long run, Rembrandt's most accomplished pupils, Lievens, Bol, Dou, Flinck, Fabritius, Maes, and Van den Eeckhout, turned away from their master's style of painting. Their work became more classical again; the irrational elements gave way to rational realities taken from nature. Examples of the Rembrandtesque, however, can be found in the work of all of them: paintings by Bol or Fabritius, for example, show Rembrandt's influence at its height. But in their later works one finds their own characteristics coming to the fore. The transition can be seen in Dou's *Old Man Cutting his Quill.* If one looks at Flinck's *Peacock* one is not immediately reminded of Rembrandt, despite the red and black chalk technique; this drawing is, strangely enough, a preparatory study for Juno's peacocks in an allegory in honor of the birth of William III (1650). Like his older contemporary and predecessor Jacob Backer, Flinck was fond of drawing with black and white chalk on Venetian gray or blue paper. Although the dating of such academic studies is difficult, it can hardly be later than 1640 and is certainly a good deal earlier than a red chalk drawing by Nicholaes Maes – a study for a painting of 1655. An anecdote! Rembrandt would never have produced one that did not have its strongly human side. Maes in his work is content with the charming exterior; and this attitude is shared by many of his contemporaries.

Only Lievens the Elder, just one year younger than Rembrandt, makes any attempt to retain something of the inward life, e.g. in his portrait of Oldenbarneveldt's servant. His portraits of the *Rev. G. Streso* and of *Descartes* penetrate even deeper beneath the surface. Van den Eeckhout, fifteen years younger than Lievens, is no less clever but he is so preoccupied with charm that one could easily attribute the drawing of a *Boy Sitting on a Chair,* illustrated here, to Fragonard.

Artists who drew landscapes were also traveling in this direction. Perhaps the least affected was Lambert Doomer, who was one of the first to see the foreign countries in which he traveled through Rembrandt's eyes and who yet retained a certain independence (France 1645/46, Switzerland 1654/55). In the work of the uncomplicated Anthonie van Borssum one can see the change-over to a more meticulous style of drawing taking place, a style that is to lead to the eighteenth-century topographical notations, with their wealth of detail. With Lievens, the case is somewhat different. His stay in England had made him conversant with Rubens's and Van Dyck's style of drawing and with their landscape motifs. Back in Holland again, after 1640, he produced a series of studies of forest outskirts that are again in the manner of Rembrandt. He was also capable of rendering his impressionistic vision in a particularly skillful and original manner through the medium of woodcuts. Something of this broad sweep is to be found again in the forceful tree groups by Abraham Furnerius, because he, too, is endeavoring to achieve a combination of grandeur and sobriety of execution. It was his brother-in-law Philips Koninck, however, who succeeded both in drawing and painting the most spacious landscapes. He was skipper of a boat traveling regularly between Amsterdam and Rotterdam; the surroundings through which his trips took him must have left their mark on his innermost being. His panoramas are perhaps the most beautiful summaries of all of an imperishable Dutch landscape, seen just as a high-flying bird might have seen it, and yet as only a man in ecstasy could have *experienced* it.

V. REMBRANDT'S YOUNGER CONTEMPORARIES

It would be a mistake to assume that all the artists of this time shared Rembrandt's vision. In Holland, as well as abroad (one thinks of Guercino, Claude Lorrain, Jordaens), there was a general tendency to evoke pictorial ideas through a combination of contrasts and suggestive lines rather than to describe them. But on the other hand attempts were being made to achieve completeness and precision. Certainly nowhere were people so sensitive to atmosphere and to intimacy as they were in Holland. While Adriaen Brouwer was acidly depicting life in the raw, the two Ostades and Jan Steen were characterizing it with a picturesquely intimate accent; and they gave an equal value to the environment. The artists were remarkably unmoved by social and human problems; but they acknowledged the glory of God in every detail and captured the beauty of light and color in the confines of a single moment. Even in a group portrait, prepared for by incisive pen studies, Adriaen van Ostade beautifully combines intimacy with variety of detail in an interior of considerable significance. His sensitive eye for all kinds of human activities never sees them as isolated phenomena but always in relation to the surroundings.

Even when occupied with religious subjects the artists of this time found it difficult to free themselves from the world in which they lived (see Isaac van Ostade's *Adoration of the Shepherds*).

How much Jan Steen owes to Isaac is shown by his bister wash drawing of an arbor at an inn; it has been executed and typified with such rapidity that one does not object to the triviality of the subject. If one looks at landscape drawings done after 1630 one is struck by the rapid chalk notations of Jan van Goyen or the brief pen-and-wash impressions of Aert van der Neer, which one can put beside the more monumental and detailed colored chalk drawings by Albert Cuyp or Van de Cappelle. Cuyp in particular, reinforcing his drawings with yellow chalk lines, displays a notable breadth of vision, sensitivity to the recession of planes and to the elementary components of the landscape. It is worth the trouble to compare them with the wide panoramas of Philip Koninck. Koninck, in creating his visionary spaces, was quite happy to use Rembrandt's suggestive style of drawing; Cuyp tried to remain faithful to nature as well as to keep the monumental conception.

Jacob van Ruisdael succeeded in evolving from the "tonal" landscapes of Van Goyen and Salomon van Ruisdael a landscape style composed with a feeling for spatial clarity, full of rich differentiations and moods of melancholy. Perhaps the melancholy was his own, such as had already been revealed in his twelve etchings (experiments of a twenty-year-old). His capacity to respond to emotion raised drawings to the level of a more universal inner life, finding an echo centuries later in the work of Goethe, for example. His paintings express this more clearly than his drawings; among the latter this strength of feeling comes out most strongly in the only church interior that he ever drew, which is nevertheless the most impressive of its time. Likewise, his view of the sands, with a few ships and the sea stretching into the distance with the sunlight glinting on it, has become an extremely poetic interpretation: it comes up to the highest aesthetic expectations of the baroque. Ruisdael wandered as far as Westphalia and, later on, Normandy. Although he made use of Scandinavian mountains as motifs he was never actually in Scandinavia. It must have been Allaert van Everdingen, who had traveled for the Trip family to their iron mine in Sweden, who provided Ruisdael with these motifs through his etchings and drawings. Van Everdingen was more of a narrator than a poet, but he sketched nature in its grander aspects magnificently. This is also true of his religious etchings, where he shows great variety despite the extremely limited number of themes. Reinier Nooms was another who wandered far, in his case to the shores of the Mediterranean. He was a capable and entertaining etcher (we know of 160 prints by him), with a gift for illustration and a great knowledge of and love for ships. He is perhaps at his purest when he limits himself to a single element and employs a simple etching technique which, as late as the nineteenth century, was to inspire the French etcher Meryon. At the other pole from Ruisdael, Meindert Hobbema, ten years younger, certainly in his drawings and paintings, and also in his choice of themes, showed an affinity with the older man. He is never dramatic but delights one by his straightforward lyricism. There is a clarity of light about all his work. His well-composed drawings are suited to the Indian summer of the golden century.

Paulus Potter, too, had he not died at the age of twenty-eight, would have played a large part in the artistic activity of this period. His style of drawing is cheerful and jaunty; a swing to a brighter way of life, to a lighter, less cerebral attitude, marks his work.

One can see the Dutch attachment to the everyday world in the portraits by Bartholomeus van der Helst, Jan de Bray, Cornelis Visscher, and Caspar Netscher, among many others, artists who faithfully and with great self-assurance portrayed middle-class townsmen, seamen, scholars, and merchants.

Roeland Roghman and Anthonie Waterloo in particular have perpetuated the beauty of countryside and town. Herman Saftleven, Van Beerstraten, Van Kessel, Van der Haagen, and many others were, like Roghman, not only sensitive to the picturesque but also to the historical. During the years 1646 and 1647, Roghman, for example, drew more than 200 castles in the provinces of Holland and Utrecht. Drawings such as these are often the source for our knowledge of these castles, which still dominated the countryside even though they were beginning to fall into decay. Waterloo, who came from Lille, was another who traveled all over Europe, journeying as far as the Baltic coast and Italy. He was fascinated by the majestic forests he saw, with their lofty trees, and by the extensive views. Although panoramic views of towns were rare at that date, he drew one of Utrecht that is striking for its topographical exactness and its poetic quality. He created harmony through his considered distribution of tonal values. Exactly how much the wandering artists learned from foreign examples cannot be determined with precision but it is quite clear that they were influenced both by the absorbing landscapes, with their fiercer quality of light, and by the ideas prevalent in foreign academies, where great importance was attached to compositional structure and the value of line. This influence can clearly be seen if one compares a pictorially observed drawing of a female figure by Gabriël Metsu with the double study of an Italian girl by Adriaen van de Velde. Despite the fragmentary nature of Van de Velde's rendering and the extra studies of hands, the accent here is nevertheless on plasticity of form and purity of contour; even in a sketch he wants to create a beautiful composition. Metsu's sketch is only a remembered image.

Netscher's style is allied to Metsu's, as one can see in a sublime portrait of a child that reminds us of Terborgh. It must be an early work because a later portrait of a girl displays the free brushstrokes of the foreign comtemporaries who came and played their part in Holland after 1660.

Cornelis Visscher and Jan de Bray remained faithful to the traditional style of drawing in their beautiful and sensitive portraits. There was no holding back the tide however; after Pieter van Laer it was probably Nicolaes Berchem who – with his drawings in red chalk – did most to pave the way for the later Italianization.

It is both striking and characteristic that most artists had various technical means at their disposal and could sketch as easily in a "classical" as in a "baroque" manner. Berchem and Jan Both were enthusiastic about the Italian landscape: their drawings, and even more their etchings, bear witness to its idyllic charm. It is surprising how these artists are able to suggest open forms by means of only a few lines. In this they are doing something new; their somewhat elder contemporary, Bartholomeus Breenbergh, still saw the opposition of light and darkness in terms of stronger contrast. His *View of Tivoli* is a clear example of the way in which a few pen lines and stipple lines have been allowed to dominate the shadowed parts, which were done in wash. This manner of drawing (also used by Pietro Testa, Guercino, Poussin, and Lorrain) continued to be widely imitated. The lawyer and artist Jan de Bisschop and his friend Constantijn Huygens Jr. exemplify this; and Van der Ulft and Terwesten carried it on well into the eighteenth century.

De Bisschop and Huygens belong to the ranks of the *dilettanti*, with a great interest in new techniques and subjects take from the antique world. De Bisschop drew from old paintings in an ink that he had invented himself. Huygens tried his hand at the pastel techniques that were coming into fashion and experimented with mezzotint (chiaroscuro) as well as collecting prints and drawings. Two army officers, the engineer Valentijn Klotz – probably from Maastricht, see his sunny group of gardens – and Josua de Grave, from The Hague, were also amateurs and began round 1667. The inventor of the fire engine, Jan van der Heyden, a civil servant (from 1669 onward), was anything but a dilettante despite the fact that his job took up a good deal of his time. His drawings, even when directed at such commercial ends as demonstrating a new fire extinguisher, far transcend the merely businesslike; in all their wealth of detail they aim at limiting and summarizing. The two Willem van de Veldes also provide practical information about ships and the technique of sailing. The father is a cool reporter of

V. Dirck de Bray, Our Lord's Instruments of Torture. 1677; woodcut; each $9\frac{1}{16}'' \times 2\frac{3}{8}''$.*
Rijksprentenkabinet, Amsterdam

what he sees; the son, equally clever at depicting rigging and armament, sees with a painter's eye; his work is more varied and less linear. A full sea with ships under a high and clouded sky calls to mind Vermeer's feeling for space in his *View of Delft*. No seventeenth-century artist so effectively rendered the bobbing of ships in a light breeze. Ludolf Backhuyzen continued to paint sea pictures in a more romantic manner after the Van de Veldes had begun working for the English.

In a country trading on such a large scale with the rest of the world, the exotic element was naturally not lacking. One thinks in this connection not only of strange animals, plants, and insects, but also of the envoys and merchants from the East, of the imported materials and goods that were admired and bought. All this gave rise to numerous scientific publications.

In cartography the Netherlands were second to none (J. Blaauw) and they took a lead in the production of books on plants and insects (Maria Sibylle Merian) to say nothing of series of illustrations (Romeyn de Hooghe and Jan Luyken, for example) with Biblical and historical themes. The richly illustrated title page lives again in the work, of, for example, Gerard de Lairesse.

This enormous activity in producing illustrations brought the art of making prints in the seventeenth century to an end. The eighteenth century was to see its continuation, with greater technical mastery and often greater polish. Woodcut technique, which in the seventeenth century was practiced skillfully and felicitously by Dirck de Bray and others, such as Lievens and Van den Valckert, no longer played a role.

All the same, if we except the prolific Jan Luyken, whose *Human Activity* and *May Morning* and numerous Biblical and historical illustrations bear witness to his imaginative purity and still point to a happy end for the seventeenth-century print, by the end of the century the dangers came to light that were to dry up the sources of inspiration and imagination. The urge to represent the truth, the quest for closely reasoned argument, took the place of naïve acceptance of what delights the heart. The century that followed was to be extremely precise as well as sensitive to the intimate, the refined, and the learned – in short a remarkable symbiosis of commerce, faith, literature and art – but naïveté had had its day.

VI. THE EIGHTEENTH CENTURY

What the preceding century had drawn and printed, the eighteenth century collected, looked at and wrote about. In the seventeenth century, outside artistic circles, the systematic collection of drawings and prints was something that rarely occurred even though there were one or two collectors of importance of whom we know. In the eighteenth century matters took a different turn. Collectors became more numerous and such men as the scholar Lambert ten Kate and the wealthy burgomaster of Delft Valerius Röver not only strove for completeness but also allowed themselves to be guided by sound taste. By the end of the century extensive collections were being formed of drawings and prints by earlier artists as well as by such contemporary masters as Van Leyden, Goll van Franckensteyn, and Ploos van Amstel. If one were to assemble the auction catalogues of this time, we would find them to contain the better part of the treasury of seventeenth-century drawings. The widespread dispersion of these began after 1800. What finally remained is important enough, but only a fraction of the original number.

Artists and collectors can be seen to have had special preferences. They liked topographical pictures, to begin with, including those with a historical slant. They enjoyed representations of animals and plants. This went together with collecting of shells, butterflies, coins, carved stones – everything that invites close inspection and study. Landscapes were very popular, but genre pieces, portraits, and Biblical and historical scenes were less sought after, except in the smaller form of book illustrations. Only toward the end of the century, in the work of Dirk Langendijk, for example, did contemporary history again become a subject of interest to artists.

It is unfair to regard eighteenth-century art in Holland as purely the expression of decadence. In relation to Europe as a whole, this country could boast of no one of the stature of Watteau, Boucher or Fragonard, Tiepolo or Guardi, Gainsborough or Reynolds. But among the countless minor artists working alongside these major figures the Dutch could hold their own, and in countries such as Germany, Scandinavia, and Spain – at least until Goya took the lead – the artistic level was not higher than in Holland. A fair comparison shows that Dutch art, through its patient dedication and its maintenance of traditional ideas, had its own recognizable character. That tradition counted for much goes without saying. That Dutch remained too unreceptive to what Paris, Venice, and London – and, later, Madrid – had to show, is a pity, but acceptable when one sees their determination to render the intimate side of life honestly. The new "design for living" too, in architecture, bright interior decoration, and carefully tended gardens, gave Holland its own individual appearance and a dignified appeal. To this very day, as one wanders along the canals of Amsterdam and many other towns, one can experience something of that eighteenth-century distinction. Paintings of this time, lacking as they are in pictorial qualities, fail to convey this distinction adequately. But the ceilings, the wall paintings in their beautifully carved frames, and the stucco all formed the background of a tranquil and cheerfully civilized way of life.

Little of this has remained intact, but numerous preliminary studies and designs were committed to paper. These can be divided into two main types that flourished alternately. At first it was mythological love scenes with large figures that were in fashion; then idealized landscapes came into favor, recalling the work of the Italianized artists and betraying the influence of Poussin and Lorrain. In this genre Glauber and the two Moucherons succeeded in achieving a personal style and an individual technique of drawing. Toward the end of the century Jurriaen Andriessen was to recreate this Arcadian genre against an airy Dutch, quasi-classical background. The first-rate water-colorist Aert Schouman drew decorative groups of birds. The stage decorator Pieter Barbiers added a genial touch to the wallpapers of his time by introducing wooded dunes into landscapes. Jacob van Strij – following the example of Albert Cuyp – suffused with sunshine his landscapes of the country around Dordrecht, his home town. His dashing style of drawing reminds us at times of Fragonard's.

Meanwhile there is Jacob de Wit, the most important mural painter and, still more, ceiling painter that Holland has produced. Because he received his training in Antwerp he was able to free himself from the traditional models in the Town Hall of Amsterdam or the somewhat later examples in The Hague (Van der Schuer, Terwesten, De Lairesse), which made the walls appear heavier rather than lighter. De Wit rendered the ceiling as an airy heaven in which allegorical figures glided, so that the room took on the appearance of a spacious banquet hall. Tiepolo's compositions were finer; there were more grandiose results to be seen in Paris or Southern Germany; but because of his originality de Wit was more than a match for the Italian Pelligrini, also working in Holland and, as far as that goes, compares favorably with James Thornhill, with his heavier ceilings. But there was no one to continue the good work after 1750, partly because of the increasing use of stucco as a medium for interior decoration. The case is quite different with regard to flower pieces, portraits, and genre pieces, which carry on the tradition of the end of the seventeenth century. Curiously enough, this cannot be said of the landscape; only at the end of the century was one to come across a large painting of a river or wood by Van Strij. There are a few additional landscape artists, such as Egbert van Drielst, Johannes Kobell, Grandjean (who died young in Italy) or Dupré, who returned from that country, and none of them reached the level of Van Goyen, Ruisdael or Hobbema. Only in views of towns is it possible to determine any definite sort of line, and here it is the work of Jan van der Heyden that remained the model. This type of drawing, however, has definitely acquired something of an individual character, and, in fact, nowhere is so large a production of topographical drawings to be found. If one includes the landscapes and sea studies (Hendrik Kobell), few as the latter are, the total is enormous.

The most prolific artists were Cornelis Pronk and Jan de Beyer, but there were dozens of others.

Paulus Constantin, Jacob Elias, and Maria la Fargue bring eighteenth-century The Hague to life. Abraham de Haen and Henricus Spilman — taking their cue from Abraham Rademaker — produce drawings for books of topographical prints. The Van Lienders make drawings of Utrecht; Hubert Pieter Schoute and Johannes Huibert Prins, of Amsterdam; Johannes van Lexmond, of Dordrecht. Lesser figures, too, such as Hendrik Keun of Haarlem, surprise us by their capacity for naive delight. Jan Hulswit, Jacob Cats and Aert Schouman were somewhat freer in their interpretations, as was certainly also the Paris-trained Reiner Vinkeles whose extensive œuvre is full of wittily and clearly observed situations on all sorts of subjects. However matter-of-fact the intention underlying all this documentation, the final results were real works of art, true landscapes, although this was not so true of paintings as of drawings. A view of a wood in water color by Paulus van Liender provides an example of this and shows that it is not only the rationalistically minded who make their mark on cultural life. One can also spot the first flutters of sentiment, including a love for revived classical ideals. Rationalism and sentimentalism make their appearance side by side, not, indeed, without passion and ridicule. The latter is to be found not only in literature but also in the graphic arts and exemplified by Cornelis Troost in the first half of the century and Jacob Smies and Jurriaen Andriessen during the French occupation.

Troost was less a moralist than an amused observer, responding readily to poignant situations and given to theatrical effects. Perhaps he pushed his subjects too often and too far in the direction of farce; his attempts at greater seriousness fall short of their mark. He has, however, a magnificent gift for characterization, and his picture of a woman done in pastel is extremely charming. His eighteenth-century sensitivity and eye for a situation enabled him to create interiors that were compositionally acceptable. He was, for instance, one of the first to paint conversation pieces in suitably light colors. Others followed him in this: Tibout Regters (1710–1768) and the younger H. Pothoven (1725–1795); a study by the latter may serve as example.

Flower pieces also continued to be produced, but they were no longer compositions clearly made up of numerous separate studies. Sketches of flower pieces are rarely met with in the seventeenth century. But now there was Jan van Huysum, creating a whole composition full of speed and movement with a few chalk lines and brush tones by means of which he achieved a supple and luxuriant unity. It deservedly brought him fame; his broad pages of richly harmonious sketches mark him out as a pioneer in a romantic genre.

Genre pieces in the style of Van Mieris and Metsu also continued to appear but, after Troost, there are few examples of such work before the last quarter of the century. A new element enters with the artistic representation of such pleasant subjects as a group of travelers in a *trekschuyt*. Our reproduction of this is by Simon Fokke, an illustrator of virtuosity who, if he lacks the sarcasm of Daumier, is not without a sense of the ridiculous. He is run pretty close by Jacobus Perkois (1736-1804) from Middelburg who knew how to give charm and character to a wide variety of types of people. Wijbrand Hendriks in Haarlem, Abraham de Lelie in Amsterdam and, somewhat later, Jacob Ernst Marcus also deserve to be mentioned.

They and many other artists pictured various wayside characters in a technique that strove for simplicity through the use of outlines for defining form. Feeling, however, takes a back seat, and Hendriks's *Distribution of Food to the Poor* — a magnificent subject that Van Gogh was later to charge with deep human feelings — remains no more than a notation that is true to nature. All the same, this shift to other subjects can fairly be regarded as a manifestation of a new interest that is not merely an interest in the picturesque. It is the beginning of a breakthrough toward concern for social injustice and misery that was to seize artists after 1800; their drawings prepare the way for Dickens and, in Holland, for Beets and his followers.

Although Dirk Langendijk (1748–1805) is still unable to break away from exact topographical representation in his numerous pictures of contemporary and military campaigns, he does manage to capture something of the savagery of war, even if he lacks Goya's intensely moving passion. Finally, this work, too, paves the way for romanticism and the dramatic experiencing of daily happenings.

With respect to this recording of all human activity the eighteenth century can point to one figure who in his final years, besides being a faithful reproducer of landscapes and an accomplished decorator, blossoms out as the most complete chronicler of his time, Jurriaen Andriessen (1742–1814). No fewer than 740 prints disclose the private and public life of his time, and it is to moments to which previous artists had only deigned to pay passing attention that Andriessen devoted himself. As director of the Amsterdam Academy he was able to influence a large number of pupils. His abbreviated style of drawing with a few penstrokes and strong contrasts of light and dark opened the eyes of many younger artists to all except the conventional contrasts and peculiarities of life: Chodowiecki, Rowlandson, and Gabriel de Saint-Aubin seldom match his gift of hitting the nail on the head.

The world of placid rest was past. The Napoleonic years increased tensions and contributed to a spiritual revolution unchaining desires that had never been known in Holland. There came about a gradual renewal of political ideas and, shortly after the liberation of the country in 1813, flashes of the romantic fire began to inspire Dutch artists too.

What we discover, looking back, was hardly noticed at the time; it is worth observing therefore that Wouter Johannes van Troostwijk, who died at the age of twenty-eight, was, despite his borrowings from Potter and Adriaen van de Velde, far in advance of his time. In his drawings especially, he is completely different from his contemporaries: see his drawing of 1808 showing the back view of a man seen against the light, which surprises one by its *mise-en-scène:* the sitter seems to have become in some inspired way the concentrated essence of his age. This feeling – which we have noted earlier in the work of Van Liender and Van Strij – finds its full expression in the few studies by Simon Krausz that have been preserved, the creations of a highly emotional artist susceptible to the psychically exceptional as manifested at certain moments by humans and animals. It is at such moments that the new century announced its arrival. People were breaking away from attempts at achieving technical completeness and were beginning to respond again to mood, seeking to hold on to it through the use of darker colors, and the sacrifice of clarity of contour to the capricious demands of particular effects.

But before we enter this new period there are two artists whom we shall have to discuss. First the English-born Charles H. Hodges (1764–1837), who in his pastel portraits, with their refined foreign elegance, created a type that was to be long imitated and developed. His lyrical nature is still better expressed in a drawing of ladies making music. In this drawing in black and red chalk he has succeeded in capturing an elegiac mood.

The second of our artists is David Pierre Giottino Humbert de Superville (1770–1840), the most unusual figure of these years. Living in a cloud of visionary images he tried to transform the pure classicism of Winckelmann's Greek world into renderings filled with medieval mysticism. One is reminded of Blake, of Füseli, of the German Koch and the other so-called Nazarenes; he is the one representative in Holland of this current. In his *Essai sur les Signes inconditionnels dans l'Art* he worked his ideas out further, examining systematically for the first time the symbolic power of lines and outlines. Only at the end of the nineteenth century were his ideas to be combined in the work of Symbolists and Pointillists. But in his own day he remained a solitary figure who got no further than the production of studies and projects. Holland, with her appetite for the real still unappeased, was not yet ripe for an art of ideas.

Again, although De Superville lacked the powerful spiritual ecstasy of Blake in his somberly exalted representation of *The Flood*, for example, this does not diminish his importance as a unique figure capable of creating – e.g. in a drawing of ice floes on the Meuse – the suggestion of a chaotic waste more vividly than any of his contemporaries could have done.

Lastly, many of the styles and ideas current during the closing years of the eighteenth century continued to be so in the nineteenth. The topographical drawings of Hulswit or Gerrit Lamberts are examples of this; Abraham van Strij in 1823 is still drawing market porters taking a rest as if Cuyp were standing at his elbow. And examples of this with respect to portrait and flower studies would not be hard to find. But in an apparently imperceptible manner different subjects were being actualized in a different coloration, with a different use of line and following different principles. The climate had changed.

VII. THE NINETEENTH CENTURY

In the nineteenth century, not only did the development toward new concepts and forms prefigured in previous centuries continue, but even older traditions still exerted influence. *Kleinmalerei* was not abandoned: topographical interest was as strong as ever; animal, flower, and genre painting as well as portraiture underwent little change. The two great movements abroad, Classicism and Romanticism, were only now and then perceptible in Holland in the transition period, which lasted till 1825 or 1830. Painstaking study of nature remained of primary interest. The eighteenth-century manner of drawing underwent only reluctant change; under Classicism it became a little more severe, sketchier, and, where Romanticism made its influence felt, more colorful. The evolution of drawing in the Low Countries fell behind. Before 1830 one can hardly speak of the existence of a Romantic school. The atmospheric landscapes by the masters of Barbizon were only discovered in Holland after 1850. A time lag of some two decades made itself felt, except with such painters as Jongkind and Van Gogh.

In spite of Holland's retreat from the forefront of artistic development, a high level of quality and a great diversity of subject matter and treatment were attained. It is difficult to make this clear to the reader in view of our limited choice of examples – far more difficult indeed for this than for preceding periods, which were much simpler to deal with. This diversity not only manifests itself in the large number lof drawings and prints but also in the techniques used. Taking its place beside etching and engraving, tithography, after 1809, began to play its part. The woodcut, an uncommon medium since the seven-eeenth century, was revived as the wood engraving. Both these techniques – together with the steel nngraving – form the basis of nineteenth-century illustration. This period is marked by the activity of trumerous engravers of reproductions; the illustrations reach artistic heights only at the hands of the ue artists.

A new facet to the art of drawing was provided by water colors. From England the technique found its way to Holland, where it reached unprecedented heights, above all when, after the middle of the century, it progressed from strokes of color to washes and so attained subtle transitions of color that have seldom been achieved elsewhere. This development in water color, and, with water color, in the entire technique of drawing, was destined to lead step by step in two seemingly opposite directions. One direction was the disappearance, the other the intensification, of outline and linear system. Intensification of lines resulted in a transformation of what was represented to the point of abstraction. If we follow this development somewhat closely, we should mention Humbert de Superville as the rather lonely representative of a kind of classicism that reappears briefly in the work of some artists who, like many of their predecessors, studied or resided in Italy (Pitloo, Teerlinck, and especially Knip).

In the distant landscapes of Andries Schelfhout and the forests of Barend Cornelis Koekkoek, who are close, yet by no means servile, followers of the trends of seventeenth-century landscape painting, a definite romantic influence is to be discerned.

We can, however, begin to speak of a truly Romantic School only when we come to Wijnand Jan Joseph Nuyen, who died at the early age of twenty-six. He succeeded in breaking away from rigid conventionalism by his imagination, mobility of touch and use of new motifs. His example was followed by Johannes Bosboom, who, especially in his church interiors, shows a sensitive awareness of the quality of light, without sacrificing feeling for architectonic space. But in that respect he was far in advance of his contemporaries, who, because of their rigid academic training, were sensitive to the other trend that arose at the same time, i.e., Realism. Besides, one might speak of a short period of Post-Classicism in which historical painting was at the height of fashion. This type of painting was especially developed in Belgium, with which strong artistic ties were maintained despite the political separation.

The reaction of members of the younger generation was not long in coming. They derived no satisfaction from an art with purely moral aims and preferred to turn to nature. Their aim was not to reproduce the correct shape or the given story but to typify an incident in daily life in a simple manner. "Truth above everything" is a clearly pronounced watchword round 1860. As examples we show some drawings by the young Willem Maris (1865) and a portrait study by August Allebé (1858). Willem Roelofs and Jozef Israëls had already led the way in this direction. Soon Gabriël, followed by the young Albertus Bilders, the three brothers Maris, and Anton Mauve, was to discover the outskirts of the Veluwe.

Although the artists of this generation also visited the forests of Barbizon and Fontainebleau, Willem Roelofs and Gabriël had a certain preference for the surroundings of Brussels, even though they regularly came over to Holland. However, the nucleus of the young school of painters was to be found in The Hague. Between 1870 and 1890 a group of artists flourished there, and attracted many others from outside. Bosboom and J. H. Weissenbruch — perhaps the most passionate painter of them all — lived there, as did Jacob and Willem Maris. Jozef Israëls, Mauve, Mesdag, and A. Neuhuys also settled in The Hague for longer or shorter periods. The sand dunes and the sea, the fisherfolk, the flat country around, cut up by its numerous canals and ditches, the lakes with their groups of trees, a bit further away, and, finally, the big rivers — all provided them with inspiration. The strange tangy atmosphere along the seashore and the moist hues of the low lying *polders* influenced their color scale and determined the mood of their rich and varied output of drawings and water colors.

The work of the second of the three brothers Maris, Matthijs, has a character all its own. After some time in Paris Matthijs Maris settled permanently in London, where his work found its culmination in a romantically tinged and dreamy delicacy. His *Royal Children* is an example. One might perhaps regard such work as the consistent outcome of ideas about nature and appearances that the artists of The Hague School — who by this time were also known as the Gray School — wanted to realize through poetic impressionism.

One figure of this period — and a very important figure — has not yet been discussed. He is the pupil of the romantic artist Schelfhout: Johan Barthold Jongkind. At first he followed in the footsteps of his fellow pupil Nuyen, and in his choice of subject matter was no different from Schelfhout or Charles Rochussen. A trip through France and a meeting with Isabey opened up new pathways. From then on, his work was on a different level. Paris and the Norman coast inspired a really astonishing fluency in his drawings and water colors. Still more amazing than his originality of technique is his originality in choice of motifs. His views of city and shore, involved as they are with his temperament, achieved a personal and novel character. Besides, his innate power of observation grew into a harmonious representation of reality informed by a curious intensity of light.

The great French landscape painters, above all Monet, acknowledged him the precursor of their own Impressionism, which unfolded shortly before 1870. In the Salon of 1882 De Goncourt noticed Jongkind's influence everywhere. In Jongkind's own country, even though he frequently visited Holland and gave a new aspect to Dutch landscape in his winter paintings and his moonlit scenes, it was a long time before he was noticed and even longer before he was appreciated. The reason for this was, perhaps, that sentiment continued for so long to be the main factor determining aesthetic appreciation. Jongkind's death in 1891 was hardly taken notice of in Holland.

Possibly the young George Breitner, who lived in Paris for seven months in 1884, became acquainted with Jongkind's skill in quickly putting a situation down on paper, for he too tried to capture life on the move, even though he continued the traditions of The Hague School insofar as he remained a tonalist. How hard he strove to capture the dynamic aspect of life is clearly shown by his sketches of streets, blocks of houses, or a building site with piles being driven into the ground. Later on, Breitner did this without the water-color hues, which, earlier in his career (see his *Saturday Evening Market in The Hague*, 1880) he had sometimes needed to present his daring and visionary evocations. Later still, he relied on black crayon alone to achieve the same results. Besides, Breitner is, because of his lively representation of contemporary events, a better historical painter than any of the professionals of the Romantic School.

It is strange that, notwithstanding Breitner's quick grasp, his drawing technique did not emancipate itself from the Dutch tradition. A contemporaneous drawing by Jozef Israëls, who was some thirty years older, looks like a more modern sequel to Breitner's academic and impressionist manner of drawing. When one sees Breitner's paintings which do not reflect anything of the tenets of *la belle peinture*, one discovers that, with all his apparently insecure and "mixed-up" licks of paint, he was yet able to convey the most subtle and immediate feelings. Toward the end of his life he was willing to surrender all form for the sake of expression. This extreme in the expression of sentiment can be taken as the utmost the nineteenth century in Holland wanted to achieve.

The same tendencies are perceptible in the work of Suze Robertson (1855-1922), the most powerful of Dutch women painters. The speed at which she worked made the lines of her drawings look like a maze of turbulence. Her drawings are generally preparatory studies for canvases that are heavily covered with paint and in which color plays a very important part. With black crayon, or, preferably, charcoal, she tried to suggest color in her drawings. She can be identified with those who, after 1880 – a time of literary innovation and economic expansion – began to form a group of realistically inclined Impressionists around Breitner in Amsterdam. In consequence, the capital gradually began to take the place The Hague had occupied previously. In Amsterdam, which was growing rapidly about this time, both the Rijksmuseum and the Stedelijk (Municipal) Museum were being built. The activities of art collectors acted as a stimulus to artistic production; and, politically and economically, there was more life here than in the quiet and sedate city of The Hague.

August Allebé, a realistic artist whom we have mentioned before, as principal of the Academie van Beeldende Kunsten (Academy of Fine Arts), influenced a group of talented pupils whose work will be discussed later. He also influenced somewhat the group that continued the traditions of The Hague School, even though they did so in their own manner.

We will close this chapter with the mention of some contemporaries. There is, in the first place, Isaäc Israëls, the son of Jozef. Isaäc Israëls, next to Suze Robertson and Breitner, was the outstanding figure of the period of about 1890. When he was just twenty years old he devoted himself to portraying the elegant life of Amsterdam's streets. He was lastingly attracted by the frivolous, volatile, and colorful, which he pursued in many towns of Western Europe and even of Indonesia. Willem de Zwart, of The Hague, is related to him in some respects. He began with similar motifs but rendered them in Breitner's naturalistic manner. Isaäc Israëls's drawing technique is closely related to Breitner's, yet is even more nervous. It hints in shorthand, as it were.

There were soon many artists who mastered Isaäc Israëls's style of drawing. We can only give one example – a sketch by Marius Bauer – a very fertile and competent etcher, especially of oriental scenes, of which he made feather-light, airy notations. These he later used as notes for his powerful fantasies of palaces and temples in water colors, oil paintings, and etchings. Even before Bauer's time the travel sketch had been rehabilitated, among others by Jacobus van Looy (Spain and Morocco). Both Van Looy and Bauer added as a new facet to Dutch art a dream of warm romanticism derived from an exotic world.

This was not all that was new around 1890. Amid all kinds of activities, to which a following chapter will be devoted, there was one that produced a real shock: the exhibitions in 1892 in The Hague and Amsterdam of the work of Vincent van Gogh.

VIII. VINCENT VAN GOGH

We have seen how, on three occasions during the course of the nineteenth century, a group of painters gave a new impetus to the art they practiced. Each generation produced its leading figures: first Bosboom and Jongkind, then Israëls, Weissenbruch, the Marises, and Mauve, who were followed in their turn by Breitner, the younger Israëls, and Suze Robertson. A fourth impetus was to follow, just before the end of the century. Acquaintanceship with the work of Vincent van Gogh was a contributory factor even at this date, and was in the twentieth century to form an important background. As far as Holland is concerned it is important to follow this development closely and in detail; while for Europe as a whole Jongkind, but even more, Van Gogh (1853-1890) are the Dutch artists who appear to be of international importance. The latter's style of drawing has an unmistakable affinity to that of Western Europe and cannot be isolated from it.

He left behind him at his early death more drawings than paintings, despite the fact that hundreds of them have been lost. Out of the total of 900 drawings we have chosen sixteen to illustrate his development. He drew throughout the whole of his life and showed even at an early age that reverence for nature that was to characterize his later works. Born at Zundert in Brabant he lived from 1870 till 1873 in The Hague, working in his uncle's art-dealing business, which took him to London from 1873–1874 and to Paris from 1874–1876. There was a quarrel, and after a crisis he returned to England and became an assistant teacher; later he moved to Dordrecht and worked in a bookshop. Finally he came to Amsterdam, where he began to study theology. When this proved a failure he followed a course for evangelists in Brussels and worked as one in the Borinage until July 1879. He was judged unsuited to this work and dismissed by the church authorities; it was then that he took up drawing in earnest. From 1880 to 1881 he was in Brussels, where he met Van Rappard, the painter.

To know something about his search to find his bearings helps us to understand a great deal about the man, as does the knowledge that it was illumination and strength that he was pursuing in his extremely varied reading, which often had a strong social accent. From this reading, he developed the art of writing letters possessed of permanent value. He was now able to link his calling as evangelist with this world of ideas by giving expression to his artistic feelings. He eagerly examined the work of others, both older and younger than he, read about them, and kept in touch with the movement in France. In this way, he became mature enough to accept the innovations of the great Impressionists and later on to join a group of younger artists (Gauguin, Lautrec, Seurat etc.) in following them. Despite his admiration for what was new, however, he never lost his respect for the old masters; in addition he was the first Dutchman to see the importance of Japanese prints for renewing modern art. His versa- tility is astonishing; all around him he found all kinds of subject matter which he proceded to work up in his own individual manner. He struggled fanatically to establish direct contact with nature. Again and again this brought him up against obstacles the surmounting of which only served to provoke the militant element in his character, releasing fresh stores of energy and stimulating his passion for his work.

After a short period of study at Etten in Brabant he went to The Hague (1882). There he learned to paint in water colors and his drawings gained in movement and in treatment of perspective. The work that resulted is full of movement, space, strong composition, and bold color. In addition Vincent tried more and more to represent things not as he saw them but as he felt them. The sketches from his period in The Hague are, as he put it himself, "laden with compassion."

After working for three months in Drente he returned to Brabant, to Nuenen (December 1883 to November 1885) where he began painting regularly. His drawing, partly influenced by theories of Delacroix, received new stimuli. The contours no longer enclose the forms but are suggested. This is particularly evident after May 1885, when after numerous preparatory studies, he completed *The Potato Eaters*.

In the pen drawings of landscapes and interiors from these later years in Holland one usually sees a structure of vertical and horizontal hatching also to be found in the etchings of Millet. But despite the innovations and despite undeniable improvement, his work, because of various external circumstances, got bogged down, and he left Holland for good, his first stop being Antwerp. There he became acquainted with Japanese wood-block prints. This had a simplifying effect on his work: he became more aware than ever of color as a means of expression; his chalk lines became more direct, more loaded, emphatic, and sudden. In March 1886 he was in Paris, where he stayed for two years with his brother Theo and where he came into direct contact with Bernard, Gauguin, Lautrec, Guillaumin, and others. These meetings, even more than his study at the Atelier Cormon, gave him new perspectives leading him beyond Impressionism, from which the other artists just mentioned were also turning away. He began to use first his reed pen and then his feather pen in a new way. He used brighter chalks; and all at once he became a complete master of form. He achieved that rapidity of drawing possessed by Oriental artists. He created still lifes, animal studies, panoramas, views of the windmills of Montmartre. The dark palette gave way to a lighter one and in his drawings the long lines of hatching were replaced by shorter strokes, at first still linked together by washes of light color. But the city stifled him. By February 1888 he was living in Arles, where his most beautiful and most expressive compositions came into being with the aid of the perspective frame that he had used as far back as his years in The Hague. A number of impressive portrait studies were created. His drawings, which in the beginning, for all their power of spatial expression, were static, were at last beginning to receive by fits and starts a dynamic character. To stippling were now added series of short lines engendering lively movement.

Under the heavy pressure of ever increasing production his work became unequal but never unexciting. His plant studies are serene. But, largely as a result of the impression that cypresses made on him, his drawings became wilder, more blazing. During this period of mental overstrain he spent a year in the hospital at St. Rémy. Afterwards, although the old pugnacity and activity were still there, creative power had undeniably been to a certain extent lost. He copied Rembrandt, Delacroix, and Millet in an attempt to regain a solid basis from which to work; he began sketching again in water color, in addition to which he succeeded, in the spring of 1889, in representing with a few curving chalk strokes the fantastic rocks of the Alpilles and the firs moving in the wind. He applied the same emotional method of drawing to such subjects as workers in the fields and peasant families. If one could only succeed in arranging the St. Rémy drawings in chronological order, one would be able to demonstrate convincingly how Vincent regained his self-confidence through drawing and enriched his style in the process. After a stay of a few days in Paris he settled down in Auvers-sur-Oise under the care of Dr. Gachet. From then on his style underwent no further changes but he took up the old themes again: portraits, cornfields, haystacks, farm workers, farms, and houses.

The illustration shows the town hall of Auvers, which reminded him of that in his birthplace. Then, unexpectedly, came the self-chosen end.

In Holland, too, his work finally began to be noticed and in a certain sense brought to a wider public. Already in Vincent's contacts with Bernard and Gauguin the importance of symbol and symbolism had repeatedly come up for discussion, a fact that is not surprising if we remember his strong literary leanings. Yet he never transforms reality into pictures that are merely symbols of concepts. His pictures are "parables" and they try by means of this pictorial language to represent life and nature with reverence and veracity. In them one can see the great love that risks all; they represent Vincent's realization of the gospel through life itself. All that he sees, paints and draws carries a message. Seen in this way, Vincent, through his individualism and his unmistakably romantic bent with its desire to abolish suffering, belongs firmly to the nineteenth century. Beside him stand the writers whose ideas possessed him: Michelet and Carlyle, Victor Hugo, and Zola, Tolstoy and Dostoevsky.

IX. SYMBOLISM, REALISM, AND THE NEW MOVEMENT

a. THE TRANSITION AFTER 1890

Vincent van Gogh's œuvre reached Holland after the death of his brother Theo in the year 1891. It was brought to the attention of a wider public in 1892 through the efforts of Theo's widow, Mrs. Van Gogh-Bonger. It was appreciated at least by a limited group of people, for since Van Gogh's departure in 1885 much had happened in Holland.

Poets and writers had reawakened people's interest in the things of the mind, especially through their writings in *Nieuwe Gids*, a periodical that had first appeared in 1885. Writers and painters made contacts with each other, and became accessible to new ideas. Not only writers and painters but musicians and architects as well (Diepenbrock, Berlage) were drawn together by the urge to satisfy their need for beauty. This enthusiastic pursuit of beauty and harmony led to a splendid late flowering of Impressionism. At the same time we witness a new urge to theorize about the aim and purpose of art.

The end-of-the-century ferment in Holland was fostered by the concomitant phenomena of the Socialist movement and the Catholic revival. The orientation of both movements was service to society. This explains how, in the initial stages, groups with widely differing outlooks on life came to work side by side. Yet, in the long run, no quest for an aesthetic form ideal can be the expression of more than one philosophy of life. The brief span in which one could envisage a unity of the arts, embracing word and image, sound and space, was to prove of singular importance. Nevertheless, as soon as form came to rank above content, the striving after common ideas had to come to grief.

The first Dutch artist capable of responding to the new ideas was Antoon Derkinderen, who was occupied between 1884 and 1888 with a monumental decorative mural representing a procession. Of particular importance are the numerous preparatory studies for the seventy persons included in the painting. Here one can already trace a reluctance to use realistic detail. This tendency is apparently not observable in the realistic portraits made by his contemporaries, but a connecting element is to be found, nevertheless, in their use of pure lines that shun picturesqueness and define the character of what they represent analytically. Examples of this are provided by drawings and lithographs by H. J. Haverman and Jan Veth. Work by the latter was to be found in monthly and weekly magazines – especially the weekly *De Kroniek* (1895–1907) – creating a point of focus for the culture of their times.

These portraits with their fine characterizations contributed to the new ideals. In order to feel the difference between Veth's approach, for example, and more pictorially conceived portraiture, one should compare his portrait of the politician and theologian, Dr. A. Kuyper, with Willem Witsen's portrait of the writer Jacobus van Looy. Veth was, after all, an art critic, a defender of advanced ideas, an art scholar, and the translator of Walter Crane's *Claims of Decorative Art*, a book that was beautifully illustrated by Willem Dijsselhof (1894) with woodcuts in a new and severe style.

The artist who more than any other expressed himself, between 1889 and 1896, by means of a wealth of gracefully decorative symbols, was Jan Toorop. Working as he did with a wide variety of techniques, he was beyond doubt the most versatile of the younger artists. The sensuous way in which he rendered nature with the aim of making his characters conveyors of ideas demanded a new lyricism and a new manner of drawing. Those he found in the art of the Pre-Raphaelites; and he enriched their vocabulary with forms borrowed from Egyptian and Oriental art. Many of his symbols had, earlier, been sources of inspiration to French, Belgian, and English literature (Medusa, Salome, Sphinx, Bride, Sunflower, etc.). Toorop returned to them, representing them as figures of melancholy menaced by fate. This literary background is clearly seen in the titles of his pictures – *Garden of Sorrows; The Three Brides; O Grave, Where Is Thy Victory?* – titles that are hard to grasp fully without calling upon the assistance of literature. The graceful and powerful line that he uses in such pictures as these he also uses in his finely composed portraits and – on a larger scale – in massive drawings of the apostles (1909–13).

There were others, too, who were driven to a more synthetic form of expression, artists such as Floris Verster (*Endegeest*, 1893) and Roland Holst (*Preaching in the Fields*, 1892), both of them strongly under the influence of Van Gogh's work. Roland Holst developed a monumental style that found its most successful application in posters and stained glass windows. For Verster and most of the others, the years shortly after 1890 would be a passing phase.

Meanwhile the art of drawing was reviving strongly. Magnificent vignettes were created; book illustration took a new lease on life; and the various graphic techniques were beginning to flourish again. The output of such graphic artists as Storm van 's Gravesande, Witsen, Bauer, De Zwart, Zilcken, and others was enormous. Van Hoytema, an extremely skillful creator of lithographs, including color lithographs, turned out animal pictures, flower pieces, and illustrations for calendars and children's books. The narrative urge that showed itself in the literature of the time was equally evident among the artists who drew according to the new formula and those who continued the Impressionism of The Hague and Amsterdam. Under the influence of foreign examples, caricatures, political especially, developed in the direction of starkly drawn types and, often, a high degree of stylization.

A large number of quieter artists worked with great dedication and concentration in a traditional and by no means incompetent manner. There is a rich harvest of sketches here, only waiting to be redeemed from an oblivion that is quite undeserved. If we illustrate the text with examples by two of these artists, we do so only with the idea of giving an impression of the artistic level that was reached and in order not to distort the over-all picture too much by drawing attention to the pioneers only. Willem Tholen made paintings, drawings, and etchings of his country, so rich in sea, lake, and river, with authenticity and individuality. Unlike the watercolorists of The Hague School, he attempted, as in his documentary drawings of such subjects as a paper mill, to give a complete impression with great simplicity and economy of line.

While Tholen was primarily a painter, Pieter Dupont was a graphic artist through and through; his copper engravings, in particular, testify eloquently to his unceasing efforts at achieving purity of form and line, by means of which he finally succeeded in freeing printmaking from its lack of pictorial restraint. It soon appeared that in woodcuts, too, similar results could be attained by arriving at a synthesis of swift impressions and considered attitudes. After pioneers like Veldheer and Nieuwenhuis had done their work, the woodcut entered a new phase. Etching followed suit, with Jessurun de Mesquita and J. J. Aarts as its most outstanding interpreters. But Dupont, who died young, was the most gifted of them all. He found his themes in Paris more than anywhere else, one of them being exemplified by his work horses by the Seine. Scenes like this also serve to illustrate what different paths artists had followed since Jongkind, fifty years earlier, had given his own pictorial rendering of the same theme.

b. *THE TRANSITION AFTER 1900*

These trends and developments of the period after 1890 took on still greater force and direction after 1900. While the turn of the century is in itself of no significance, the fact that the international exhibition in Paris was a triumph for *Art Nouveau* is important, particularly for the various branches of applied art. In addition, the building of the Amsterdam Exchange by Berlage, completed in 1904, paved the way for a common life of architecture and the plastic arts. Generally speaking, one would like to date the turning point at about 1907, one year after the death of Cézanne, whose work was by that time attracting a great deal of attention. From this time on, in Holland, it was possible to speak of Expressionism and Fauvism, on the one hand, and of Cubism and – somewhat later – Futurism and Abstract art on the other. Under the influence of Pointillism and Divisionism many a painter's palette became lighter in tone. Jan Toorop, always ready to absorb new ideas, was the most rigorous and consistent in his application of the technique of stippling. The technique was converted into something more dynamic that nevertheless kept its strong intensity of light. This can be seen in Johan Thorn Prikker's renderings of Limburg landscapes (about 1900), for example, which succeed in evoking emotional spatial hints by their use of separate short kaleidoscopic strokes. It seemed a logical evolution, but it did not satisfy for long; the general urge toward a greater forcefulness of expression compelled the artist to let contours once more dominate his compositions. Indeed, before 1914, all the various aspects were to be seen of the struggle to make neither configuration nor space but rhythm the decisive element. Artists no longer seemed capable of handling space.

They were no longer satisfied with the rendering of the Impressionist's accidental and instantaneous aspect of nature but were aiming at the establishment of what might be called the salient viewpoint or preferably the synthesis of a series of salient viewpoints; concepts began to play a more important part than the raw data of vision. In essence, the struggle was old, but its character had been changed by all those twentieth-century factors that speed up, revolutionize, and disintegrate life. The discoveries made by psychology deepened man's knowledge of mankind, making him more receptive to archetypal patterns and primitive art.

The generation that came to the forefront after 1900 with an accent entirely its own was that of Piet Mondrian (born 1872), the most progressive of all his contemporaries, although it is also the generation of Bart van der Leck (born 1876) and Kees van Dongen (born 1877), both of whom were under the influence of French artists such as Steinlen. Van der Leck's *Street Scene* (1906) is a remarkable document, showing as it does a new manner of composition which he later pursued to its logical consequences. Van der Leck's starting point was Van Gogh; Van Dongen's was orginally Isaäc Israëls and Breitner, until he came into contact with the Fauves in Paris, after which his style of drawing was primarily devoted to a colorful expression of the typical. From time to time he returned to Rotterdam, to make surprising views of the river there. These drawings are more emotional and altogether freer than any by his contemporaries.

While Van Dongen grouped himself with the Fauves, the younger generation had its eye more on Cézanne (Lodewijk Schelfhout); Seurat (Dirk Nijland); Van Gogh, Gauguin (Jan Sluyters); and on Picasso (Leo Gestel). In the work of all Cubism and Expressionism are intermingled, but nowhere do we find a complete absence of traces of the visible world – that remained a reality for them. Sluyters is more a painter of portraits and human figures. Schelfhout stuck to landscapes – partly as a result of his long stay in Provence. Nijland and Gestel, in their different ways, both assimilated Seurat, Nijland reverting to a terse, figurative realism that is sometimes full of humor, Gestel, with his own mixture of Cubism and Futurism, succeeding in drawing portraits, like the one illustrated, that allow us to experience to the full the tensions of those pre-World War I years. Later on, in 1914, in Majorca, he reached a high point in his career; he created in light pastel shades cheerful Cubist harbor views and orchards that remain firmly controlled by virtue of their rhythmic planning. With Gestel, therefore, one can speak of an expressive Cubism. He tried to arrive at what is essential by the use of forms and colors that are approximations of the inner life. With Sluyters, the illustrative character of his early style of drawing disappeared after 1905. His studies of cafés and nightclubs – then still a new phenomenon in Holland – have a sensitive and at the same time sensual quality about them; they are above all acute psychological analyses.

Alongside these younger artists, others – Toorop, Derkinderen, Roland Holst, Van Konijnenburg, who center their attention on essential artistic values – were carrying on with their work. Van Konijnenburg by rejecting Impressionism and by theorizing in his book *The Aesthetic Idea* (1916) exerted influence when, not unlike Mondrian, he worked out theories based on the opposition between mind and matter, an opposition which he resolves into a unity in "the representation," the aim of which is to express "the ethical element of the aesthetic idea."

Mondrian, who was originally a theosophist, was no less ethically minded. He slowly worked his way toward the certainty that he was looking for. Thanks to Sluyters, he freed himself from Impres-

VI. S. Jessurun de Mesquita, Zebra. 1912; woodcut; $10\frac{13}{16}'' \times 16\frac{5}{16}''$.
Stedelijk Museum, Amsterdam

sionism. Toorop led him to a new synthesis of Luminism and Divisionism. The hardening of his structure shows in tree studies (1910). In Paris, and, later, in Domburg (Zeeland), his motifs began to become so abstract that by 1914 a completely two-dimensional structure had been raised to another level of existence. He himself saw it as follows: "In order to approach the spiritual in art one must do with a minimum of reality, for reality is opposed to spirituality."

It would be wrong to regard Mondrian's abstract formulations as the unequivocal end point in the development of Dutch drawing. Subsequent development has given a different picture. The road leading to abstract, and later on, to non-figurative art can be seen to lead in only one of the possible directions in which artists can travel, although it is certainly an essential one offering a widely varying range of possibilities. But at the same time, the Indian summer of Impressionism after 1900 provided a rich and long-lasting harvest; and Expressionism, too, gave signs of its increasing vitality and capacity to inspire. By 1914, however, a terminal point had been reached. With the entry of the German armies into Belgium, the First World War broke out and Holland became isolated. When at last the fire had been put out and only the last smoldering embers were left, much could be seen to have been destroyed and uprooted. After 1918, life began slowly and painfully to renew itself and regain strength; an unmistakably new climate developed that tried to accomodate forms and ideals, both old and new. A period began that has still not come to its end and that has not yet found its place in history.

TECHNICAL DATA

PAPER AND WATERMARKS. The manufacture of paper in Europe began about 1150. For a long time thereafter it was scarce. In the fourteenth and fifteenth centuries, and even later, parchment was also used. The color of the paper used is important, especially with chalk drawings.

By watermark is understood the trademark that the maker of the paper gave to his product. Papers and watermarks can be dated back to the end of the thirteenth century, although often only approximately. The identification of a watermark gives one a *terminus post quem*, i.e., the drawing concerned can have been made only after the date of paper and watermark.

DRAWING TECHNIQUES. With respect to technique, drawings may be divided into six groups: 1. pen-and-ink drawing, 2. pen-and-wash drawing, 3. brush drawing, 4. metalpoint, 5. drawing in soft materials such as charcoal and chalk, 6. mixed techniques.

PEN-AND-INK DRAWING. This oldest and most widely used technique depends for its effect on three factors: the drawing instrument, the ink, and the paper.

A sharpened reed has done duty as a pen, from ancient times and, since 1100, the goose quill has also been used widely. Later on, harder quills make their appearance—swan, raven, and woodgrouse quills—enabling finer and more detailed work to be carried out. After 1830 the steel nib comes into use. Three of the most widely used inks are gall-nut (black), the so-called India ink (gray), and bister (brown). As early as the sixteenth century people had begun to draw with other, colored inks. After 1800 sepia (gray-brown) and synthetic inks come into use. In the course of time most inks lose their characteristic color, because of oxidation or fading, and it is often impossible to determine the ink used. Modern descriptions of old drawings usually indicate the ink according to the present color. The sixteenth-century draughtsmen and engravers, in particular—Lucas van Leyden, Maerten van Heemskerck and, later, Goltzius—made frequent use of pen-and-ink drawing without wash. An example is provided in Plate 13, which has been done in brown ink with a (goose) quill.

PEN-AND-WASH DRAWING. This old and well-tried method consists of working with a brush over a pen-and-ink drawing. The amount of dilution of the ink gives rise to a range of tone values. Rembrandt is the undisputed master of the pen-and-wash drawing. The drawing reproduced as Plate 63 had been done first in brown ink with a (goose) quill and then with the brush.

BRUSH DRAWING. The name speaks for itself. The drawing is done with the point of a brush. This technique is characteristic of Venetian drawings of the fifteenth and sixteenth centuries. It was Albrecht Dürer who introduced it into the North. Bosch's *Entombment* (Pl. 3) has been drawn in brush point and wash in gray ink over a sketch in black chalk (or charcoal).

A *gouache* is a brush drawing in opaque water color. The pigment is mixed with distilled water and bound to the paper with gum or glue. Gouache is found as early as Dürer's famous studies of animals, plants, and landscapes.

A *water color* is a brush drawing in water color. Although one can point to various examples of this technique in the sixteenth and seventeenth centuries, it was only after 1750 that the water color really came into its own as an independent art form. The drawings by Goltzius (Pl. 22) and Gerbrandt van den Eeckhout (Pl. 90) can be considered, therefore,

to be examples from the prehistory of water color. The technique itself really belongs more to painting than to drawing. The Impressionists and Post-Impressionists saw in water color an excellent medium for realizing their objectives. Holland has produced many excellent water-color artists, both past and present. A few are the somewhat conservative Bosboom, and, later, Jongkind (Pl. 174-178), Breitner (Pl. 179-180), and Sluyters.

METALPOINT. Forerunner of the pencil, the metalpoint was widely used in the fifteenth and sixteenth centuries, especially the leadpoint and the still harder silverpoint. Copper, brass, and gold are other drawing metals of which mention is found. Because metalpoint leaves no permanent impression on ordinary paper but does on a hard surface, the procedure is to prepare parchment with hard coating of glue and (usually colored) powdered bone. In earlier times parchments prepared in this way, and resembling ivory tablets, were bound together as drawing albums. Dürer's sketchbook, in which he drew in silverpoint during his journey through the Netherlands, is the best known example. In the Northern Netherlands it was particularly Goltzius and his pupil Jacob de Gheyn II who used this technique. One should distinguish between the metal leadpoint and the stone graphite point that later became the pencil. Graphite points (*plumbum hispanicum*) were in use as writing material as early as the sixteenth century. In the seventeenth century they were often also used in the Netherlands for drawing (Pl. 35). Nicolas Jacques Conté (1755-1805) is regarded as the inventor of the pencil. By mixing graphite and clay under heat he succeeded in producing a material whose hardness could be controlled.

SOFT DRAWING MATERIALS. Those most often used are charcoal, and black, red, and white chalk. A distinction is made between ordinary charcoal and oiled charcoal, and between the older, natural chalks (black rock-chalk, red clay earth, white pipe clay) and the more recent artificial chalks such as crayons and pastels. Charcoal is one of the oldest drawing materials. It was used for first sketches over which the picture was often redrawn in another technique (Pl. 3). After 1500 charcoal drawings were often fixed by being sprayed with a fixative consisting of, for example, clear shellac dissolved in spirits. Black and red chalk techniques reached full development in Italy at the beginning of the sixteenth century. In the Northern Netherlands Lucas van Leyden (black chalk) and Maerten van Heemskerck (red chalk) first mastered this technique fully. During the course of the sixteenth century, chalk began to be used more and more. Goltzius, a man of many parts, is credited with being one of the first to use two chalk techniques that only later were to come into general use: pastel drawing and drawing à *deux* or à *trois crayons*. Pastel drawing, which Lille-born Wallerant Vaillant (1623-77) was one of the first to shine at, is actually more a painting technique. This process consists of painting (rubbing) with a rolled-paper stomp and dry paint. At the beginning of the eighteenth century Watteau brought this technique à *deux et* à *trois crayons* (combinations of two or three sorts of chalk on white or colored paper) to heights previously unattained.

PRINTS. In popular language a print means a picture. The term can refer to any printed representation or, with less justification, to a drawing. In the history of art a print is understood to mean the end product of various graphic printing processes, excluding photographic techniques. The different kinds of prints are classified as follows:

I. *Relief prints:* woodcut and wood engraving.

II. *Intaglio:* engraving and etching, with their allied techniques (drypoint, mezzotint, stippling, crayon engraving, pastel engraving, aquatint, and soft-ground etching.

III. *Surface prints:* Lithography.

RELIEF PRINTS. In a relief print the outlines of the picture to be reproduced, i.e. the lines that are inked, project beyond the uninked background.

Woodcut. The drawing is made on wood sawn with the grain. All wood that does not form part of the drawing is cut out. The part remaining—which, consequently, stands higher than the rest—is spread with a thick ink. When the block is printed on paper the raised part produces an inked image and the part cut away leaves uninked paper. The earliest woodcuts in the Netherlands date from the beginning of the fifteenth century; in the North Netherlands book illustration reached its peak after 1480 (cf. Pl. I). *Chiaroscuro woodcuts* were printed in two or three colors from separate blocks used one after the other. The earliest color prints appeared after 1520 in Germany and Italy, and subsequently also in the Netherlands (Lievens, Pl. IV) and elsewhere.

Wood engraving. This nineteenth-century process is based on the same principle as the woodcut but the drawing is done on boxwood cut across the grain, and the material is worked with the sharpened chisel-point of the engraving tool, the burin. The possibilities for detailed work are much greater than with woodcuts and the result is finer and subtler.

INTAGLIO PRINTS. With an intaglio print the outlines of the picture to be reproduced, i.e. the lines that are inked, are hollowed out.

Engraving. The design is pricked in a copper plate by means of a graver. Sometimes plates of zinc, steel, silver, or gold are used. The grooves that have been scored out are filled with ink, after which the copper plate, which has first been thoroughly cleaned, is pressed into damp paper with the aid of a press. For this an engraving press is used with two rollers through which the copper plate with the dampened paper can be passed under pressure. The arrays of lines parallel to or crossing one another that can be observed on an engraving are called hatchings. Plastic effects, such as contrasts of light and shadow, are usually effected in an engraved picture by varying the spacing of the hatching or by altering the thickness of the hatchings in places. The engraving is younger than the woodcut. The technique was perfected towards the middle of the fifteenth century, particularly in Germany. The earliest Netherlandish engravings were made in the last quarter of the same century (cf. Pl. 1). In the sixteenth century two masters, in particular Lucas van Leyden (cf. Pl. 7, 8, 9) and Hendrick Goltzius (Pl. 20), brought the art of engraving to a previously unknown degree of perfection. In the seventeenth and eighteenth centuries the engraving was to a very large extent superseded by the etching and other techniques. It was only at the beginning of the twentieth century that it again attracted new adherents (P. Dupont, J. J. Aarts).

Etching. In an etching the drawing is not scored out of the plate but eaten out by acid. The polished copper or zinc plate is covered with a so-called etching ground, which is a varnish consisting of a mixture of resin and wax or asphaltum. The etching ground is heated and the design drawn in the resulting tacky substance with an etching needle, so that the metal is laid bare wherever the lines are drawn. After the back and sides have been provided with a protective layer of varnish the plate is immersed in the etching bath, usually a solution of hydrochloric or nitric acid. The acid bites the metal away

wherever it has been drawn on. When certain parts have been sufficiently etched the etching ground is washed off. The plate and the lines that have been etched enough can then be re-covered with etching ground and the process repeated to a greater depth. This is repeated until proofs, which can be taken after every etching, show the desired result to have been attained. Printing is done, as with engravings, by means of a press. The advantage possessed by the etching over the engraving is that the artist can draw freely in the etching ground; the engraving involves scoring of hard metal with a burin, tying him far more to the demands of his instrument and his material. The earlier etchings were made in Germany at the beginning of the sixteenth century. In the Netherlands at that time etchings were few and far between (Lucas van Leyden). It was only in the seventeenth century that etchings became general. The neat little etchings of Buytewegh were made at the beginning of the century (Pl. 44, 47); later it is Seghers, Rembrandt and the latter's pupils who stand out (cf. Pl. 48-53, 75-82) as masters of this technique.

Drypoint. The lines are scratched in the metal with a very sharp needlepoint, after which the plate is not etched but printed "dry," like an engraving. The scratching results in a projecting edge, the burr, which on printing lends the drypoint line an expressive, velvety character. This process is mostly applied in combination with the etching technique. Rembrandt, from 1640 on, frequently used the drypoint as an independent technique.

Mezzotint. Here the first and most important concern is the uniform roughening of the surface of the copper plate. This is achieved by rocking a fine-toothed tool, or rocker, over the plate. The plate that has been roughened in this way, if inked and printed, presents as a result a velvety black surface. The next stage is to scrape a design into the plate; the appropriate rough parts are rendered completely smooth with a burnisher. On printing, these parts absorb no ink, so that they appear white on the paper. The more burnishing is done, the more white will appear in the print, and vice versa. Mezzotint, stippling, crayon engraving, and pastel engraving are the tonal engraving processes. The earliest mezzotint print, made by Ludwig von Siegen, dates from 1642. In the second half of the seventeenth century there were several Netherlanders who made use of this technique, among them Abraham Blooteling, Jan and Nicolaas Verkolje, and Cornelis Dusart. It reached its real zenith, however, as a technique for reproduction, in the eighteenth century, especially in England.

Stipple engraving. The plate is worked with an engraving iron, an etching needle, or a toothed wheel called a roulette. No lines are pricked, only dots. Johannes Lutma the Younger (1624-89) made some remarkable portraits using this technique.

Crayon engraving. For this a roulette is used and the mattoir (matting wheel) that leaves a track behind it looking on the print like a line made with chalk. This technique was much used during the eighteenth century, especially in France. In this way drawings by masters such as Boucher were reproduced in the original, often red, shade.

Pastel engraving. Here the same working methods are applied as in crayon engraving, but the printing is done in colors from separate plates. This technique, too, made great headway in the eighteenth century, again particularly in France. More or less the same result can be achieved by means of another intaglio process in color in which different colors are applied to—actually painted on—a single plate. The process has to be repeated after every printing. The learned Johan Teyler from Nijmegen (d. 1712) experimented with the printing of colored line engravings.

Aquatint. Aquatint and soft-ground etching are tonal

etching processes. The outward character of the aquatint can best be compared with wash drawing or with water color. The plate is first provided with a porous ground. This is done by covering it evenly with finely powdered resin, after which the plate is heated so that the grains on it melt and fuse together. Another method is to pour over the plate a solution of powdered resin in alcohol (spirit ground). When a plate treated in this manner is dipped in an etching bath and the etching ground removed, a very finely stippled surface results after inking and printing. The determining factor is the length of time the plate is exposed to the corrosive bath. If this is brief, the plate is lightly bitten, and, after it has been inked and wiped, prints will show a very light tonality. Those parts of the picture that he wants to leave white the artist covers with a protective coat of varnish before he starts on the first etching bath. After the first print has been made the plate can again be given a porous ground and etched again, with sections that need protection being stopped by varnish. The process is repeated until the desired result has been obtained. Aquatint is an eighteenth-century technique first successfully applied in 1768 by a Frenchman, J. B. le Prince. In the Netherlands, Ploos van Amstel (d. 1798) made use of this method of working in his imitations of drawings by old masters. Various other methods are known of making an etching ground porous. One of them entails the abrasion of an ordinary etching ground with sandpaper or emery powder.

Soft-ground etching. Another tonal etching method, the result of which resembles a brush or chalk drawing, is soft-ground etching. The plate is furnished with an etching ground, namely the usual varnish mixed with tallow. After being heated and allowed to cool the etching ground becomes soft and tacky. A thin sheet of paper with a somewhat rough surface is laid on top and drawn on in chalk. When removed the paper takes with it enough varnish from the etching ground for granulated lines to be exposed. In this way, after etching and printing, one gets an effect similar to crayon engraving, yet achieved by completely different means.

States. Every stage in the etching or engraving of a copper plate that is recorded by means of a print is called a state. We speak of the successive states; and they are usually numbered. There are usually few prints of a first state. However, because as many prints can be made of an early as of a late state, a low number is no guarantee of high quality. The first state usually carries the address, i.e. the name of the publishing firm. When the plate is worn out, the address is usually erased, so that the firm is no longer responsible for any later printing that may possibly occur. While he is working on a plate an artist may make test prints in order to check the results of his alterations. These prints are then, of course, mirror images. If he considers it desirable to see the image correctly he runs the wet proof through the press with a white sheet of paper and thus obtains an image that corresponds with the original drawing. Such a print is called a *contre-épreuve*.

SURFACE PRINTS. One speaks of a surface print when the outlines of the picture, and thus the lines that are inked, lie on the same level as the material in which they are made.

Lithography. The commonest form of surface printing is lithography. This technique is based on the natural principle that water and grease will not mix. Lithographs in their simplest form are made as follows. A drawing is made on porous stone with a specially prepared greasy chalk. The type of limestone that lends itself best to this purpose is the so-called Solnhöfer stone, discovered accidentally by Senefelder in 1796. For a chalk drawing the surface of the stone is ground so that it becomes as finely grained as drawing paper. The stone is then well moistened and gone over with an inking roller (brayer) made of rubber. The printing ink, which consists of pigment mixed with oil, is rejected by the wet stone but accepted by the greasy chalk. The drawing on stone thus obtained can be printed a number of times. The drawing can be lightly etched with a solution of gum arabic and very dilute nitric acid. By this means the greasy chalk becomes more closely compacted with the stone, and the blank stone, by the action of the acid, becomes less absorptive of grease. After the first light etching the drawing is rubbed with fine resin, which gives the chalk greater resistance during the stronger etching to follow. The stone is then cleaned with water, rubbed with a thin solution of gum, and allowed to stand for some hours, after which the gum is washed off. The chalk is dissolved in turpentine and removed; the stone is kept wet with a damp cloth; and the drawing apparently disappears, although not actually, because the pigment is dissolved while the grease remains. For printing, a lithographic press is used. The stone and the paper (which is first covered with a frisket, or protective paper sheet with a window where the image will come) are passed under an adjustable heavy drum which presses the paper firmly against the stone. The number of prints obtainable from a well-prepared stone is considerable. As well as drawing directly on the stone one can draw on paper and then transfer the representation to the stone by means of a press. This principle leads to countless variations that can be applied with the etching and engraving techniques already discussed in the section on intaglio. Unlike what happens with the wood-cut etching or engraving, the treatment that the lithographic stone undergoes once the drawing is on it is always the same. Accordingly, the artist can not, as he can in the case of an etching, for example, alter the result of his work. In an engraving the engraver may or may not work on the product of his own imagination, but the fact will usually be recorded in the inscription. With an etching the draughtsman (inventor) and the etcher are normally one and the same person. The lithograph, however, is always signed with the name of the artist, regardless of who has done the printing.

COLLECTIONS

THE COLLECTING OF DRAWINGS IN HOLLAND. A large number of artists, including Rembrandt and Jan van de Cappelle, are known to have amassed considerable collections of drawings and prints, partly because of the sheer desire to collect, partly because they wanted them as study material. Toward the end of the seventeenth century, a considerable increase in activity in the collector's field can be seen to have taken place in the Netherlands, particularly among rich private persons. Many print rooms owe their showpieces to the flair and the protective appreciation of art collectors such as J. P. Zoomer (1641-1724), N. A. Flinck (1646-1723), or Valerius Röver (d. 1739). It was in Amsterdam that the important collections were auctioned and disposed of. In the eighteenth century, especially, a lively market developed there as a result of which the younger generations were given the chance to form new cabinets of drawings. It was at this time that C. Ploos van Amstel (1726-98), an artistically minded Amsterdam wood merchant, and the bankers Goll van Franckenstein built up their celebrated collections, which were both quantitatively the best that had ever been seen in Holland. J. G. Verstolk van Soelen (1776-1845) and G. Leembruggen (1801-65) were their worthy successors. The King of Holland, William II, was another who earned his spurs as connoisseur of old drawings. Sad to say, however, his Raphaels that had come from Sir Thomas Lawrence's fine collections were later sold again to England. One of the most noteworthy collectors after 1850 was Jacob de Vos Jbzn. When his collection of drawings came under the hammer in 1883, the National Print Room (Rijksprenten-kabinet) in Amsterdam was one of the eager buyers. The age of the permanent, public print room had begun and this went hand in hand with an increasing severe reduction in private collections and in the art market as a whole.

There are a number of twentieth-century collectors who have considerably enriched Dutch national art treasures and may be mentioned here: C. Hofstede de Groot, the art historian who was the first to catalogue Rembrandt's drawings and who in 1930 bequeathed a large part of his collection, including sixty-five Rembrandt drawings, to the Rijks-prentenkabinet in Amsterdam, while another part went to the Museum van Oudheden in Groningen in 1931; F. Koenigs, the Haarlem collector and connoisseur, whose collection was acquired by the Museum Boymans during World War II with the help of the art collector D. G. van Beuningen; and A. Welcker of Amsterdam whose collection recently signified an important extension to the possession of the University of Leiden.

Private Dutch collections of drawings. Almelo: E. ten Cate H. Ezn.; Amsterdam: P. de Boer, P. Brandt, Erven W. J. R. Dreesmann, C. P. van Eeghen, J. Q. van Regteren Altena; Goor: D. Hannema; Laren: V. W. van Gogh; Leiden: L. J. J. G. Vosmaer; Paris: Frits Lugt; Vorden: Mrs. A. J. H. J. A. Gatacre-de Stuers, A. Staring.

THE COLLECTING OF PRINTS IN HOLLAND. An interest in drawings went hand in hand, naturally, with an interest in prints. Many collectors of drawings, such as Ploos van Amstel, C. Josi, Verstolk van Soelen, to mention a few, also had large collections of prints. Michiel Hinloopen (1619-1708) owned a rare collection of etchings by Seghers; P. Cornelis Baron van Leyden built up an extensive collection of Rembrandt etchings in the eighteenth century; both collections found their way in the nineteenth century to the Rijks-prentenkabinet, as did the fine collections of Dutch historical prints belonging to Frederik Muller. The print room of the Museum Boymans only grew to its full stature in this century; in 1923 the collection of A. J. Domela Nieuwenhuis was acquired; but the real cornerstone of the print room's possessions is the valuable legacy of J. C. J. Bierens de Haan, who, in 1951, bequeathed to the Museum Boymans his very complete collection, consisting largely of Dutch prints of before 1850. The basis of the print collection in the University of Leiden print room is formed by the legacy of J. T. Royer, who died in 1814, and the collection of N. C. de Gijselaar, acquired in 1853. In 1947, on the initiative of a number of private collectors in Holland, the "Amsterdamse Prentkring" was formed, the members of which form a closed society of collectors of prints and drawings with the aim of facilitating personal contacts and the furthering of judgment through talks and meetings.

PRINT ROOMS IN HOLLAND. "Print room" is a traditional and really inadequate name for a collection of drawings, engravings, etchings, and other products of graphic processes. Drawings and prints can be viewed in the following Dutch museums and institutions: Amsterdam: Rijksmuseum (Rijks-prentenkabinet), Stedelijk Museum, Rembrandthuis, Museum Fodor, Gemeente-archief; Arnhem: Gemeentemuseum; Dordrecht: Dordrechts Museum; The Hague: Gemeentemuseum; Groningen: Museum voor Oudheden; Haarlem: Teyler's Museum, Gemeente-archief; Leiden: Prentenkabinet der Rijksuniversiteit; Otterlo: Rijksmuseum Kröller-Müller; Rotterdam: Museum Boymans; Utrecht: Centraal Museum. Besides what is contained in the archives at Amsterdam and Haarlem, many other, particularly topographical drawings, are to be found in the Rijksarchief in The Hague and in most of the municipal and provincial archives.

NOTES ON THE REPRODUCTIONS

In this list the captions to the reproductions have been supplemented by notes. In addition, some information has been furnished about the artists whose work features in the book.

In the captions to the reproductions an asterisk after the measurements indicates that the work has been reproduced in its true size.

NORTH NETHERLANDS SCHOOL. C. 1485.

1 *Landscape with Rocks.* Woodcut. Made at Haarlem; illustration for Bartholomeus Anglicus's *Boeck van den proprieteyten der dinghen*, Chapter XVI: Van den costelicken ghesteenten, geprint van mi Meester Jacop Bellaert, gheboren van Zerixzee, 1485 (op den heylighen Kerstavont) Haerlem. The book described the creation of the world of "living things," both animal and vegetable, and contains eleven illustrations.

CORNELIS ANTHONISZ. B. Amsterdam, c. 1500; d. 1553. His woodcuts were mostly done between 1527 and 1553.

II *The Devil of Cards and Wine.* Woodcut. Inscribed with monogram. Printed about 1540. The devil of cards and wine is represented as a man with the head of a pig, who holds a wine can in his left hand and with his right waves a sword over his head. On his head are vine leaves interspersed with playing cards; little winged devils are flying out of his snout. The upper part of his body is encased in a wine barrel which serves him as armor.

WERNER VAN DEN VALCKERT. B. c. 1590; d. c. 1635. Probably born and died in Amsterdam, where he worked for many years.

III *Plato.* Woodcut. Inscribed "W.V.V. Inv. Plato. 1620." There is another copy (chiaroscuro) in Vienna. Companion piece to a *Charon* made in the same year.

JAN LIEVENS. B. Leiden, 1607; d. Amsterdam, 1674.

IV *Border of the Wood.* Woodcut. Inscribed "J.L." Made after his return from Antwerp (1644).

DIRCK DE BRAY. B. Haarlem, c. 1620; d. Haarlem or Brabant, after 1678. Brother of Jan de Bray (see Plate 120).

V *Our Lord's Instruments of Torture.* Woodcut (tone blocks black and red). Inscribed "f.D.d. Braij." Above the cross is the inscription: "Jesu van Nazaret, Koning der Jooden" (Jesus of Nazareth, King of the Jews). A signed preparatory study is dated 1677-3/21.

S. JESSURUN DE MESQUITA. B. Amsterdam, 1868; d. Germany, 1944.

VI *Zebra.* Woodcut. Made in 1912.

MASTER I. A. (M.) OF ZWOLLE. Worked in Zwolle between 1460 and 1490.

1 *The Madonna and Child with Cherries.* Engraving. Inscribed with monogram "IAM" and maker's mark, a goldsmith's drill. Also "zwll" (Zwolle). Datable about 1485. Other copies in print rooms in Vienna and London.

HIERONYMUS BOSCH. B. 's-Hertogenbosch, c. 1450; d. 1516.

2 *Tree-man.* Pen and brown ink. Signed (later) "Bruegel." Related to a representation on the right wing of *The Garden of Delights* in the Prado, Madrid.

3 *The Entombment.* Brushpoint in gray over black chalk or charcoal, with gray washes. Signed on sarcophagus, "IHERONIMUS BOSCH." Study for a sculpture in wood.

4 *Monsters.* Pen and brown ink on reddish paper. Signed (by a later hand) "Jero Bosch." On the verso is a lobster-like beast such as is also found on a grisaille representing

The Wickedness of Mankind in the Museum Boymans, Rotterdam.

ALLAERT DU HAMEEL. B. 's-Hertogenbosch (?), c. 1449; d. 's-Hertogenbosch or Louvain, c. 1509. Engraver and architect, active, among other places, in Louvain (1494-1503).

5 *The Raising of the Brazen Serpent.* Engraving. Inscribed "bosche" ('s-Hertogenbosch), and also with monogram "A" and printer's mark. The Old Testament representation (Numbers 21: 8-9) was regarded as a prefiguration of the crucifixion of Christ.

JACOB CORNELISZ VAN AMSTERDAM, also called VAN OOSTSANEN. B. Oostzaan, before 1470; d. Amsterdam, 1533.

6 *Scenes from the Life of the Virgin.* Woodcut. Signed with monogram and inscribed with engraver's mark. *Joseph at Work during the Flight into Egypt, Return from Egypt, The Funerary Procession,* and *The Assumption of the Holy Virgin* form part of a series of scenes from the life of the Virgin. This series consists of seven pages comprising twenty-seven subjects; one of the pages bears the date 1507. Earliest dated woodcut by this master. Only copy extant.

LUCAS VAN LEYDEN. B. Leiden, 1489 or 1494; d. 1533. Most likely born in 1489. Journeys to Antwerp (1521) and Middelburg (1522?).

7 *The Raising of Lazarus.* Engraving. Inscribed with monogram "L." Made about 1507, shortly before the earliest dated print by Lucas (1508).

8 *Ecce Homo.* Engraving. Inscribed with monogram "L" and the year "1510."

9 *The Joys of this World and Mary Magdalene.* Engraving. Inscribed "1519." A number of scenes from the worldly career of Mary Magdalene inspired by miracle plays of shortly after 1500. In the foreground can be seen the saint herself, with a halo, dancing with a young man to the strains of flute and drum; in the middle distance she is shown at the hunt pursuing a deer; in the background, high in the clouds, her ascension appears, on a much smaller scale.

10 *A Girl Reading.* Black chalk. Inscribed with monogram "L." Narrow addition at the top. Dated about 1520.

11 *Portrait of a Young Man.* Black chalk. Inscribed with monogram "L" and the year "1521." Drawn in Antwerp under Dürer's influence. Related drawings in the Print Rooms in Paris, Stockholm, Florence, London, Oxford, and Weimar.

12 *Man Drawing.* Black chalk. Inscribed with monogram "L," about 1521 or a little later.

MAERTEN VAN HEEMSKERCK. B. Heemskerck, 1498; d. Haarlem, 1574. Journeyed to Italy.

13 *Obelisk of St. Peter's near St. Peter's and Santa Maria delle Febre.* Pen and brown ink. This drawing and our No. 15 derive from one of the sketchbooks originated during the master's stay in Italy (1532-36). A large number of such drawings, once in the possession of Pieter Saenredam, are now preserved in the Print Room in Berlin.

15 *Palatine with Colosseum in the Background.* Pen and brown ink. See note to No. 13.

JAN VAN SCOREL. B. Schoorl, 1495; d. Utrecht, 1562. Worked in Haarlem as well as in Utrecht. Journeyed among other places to Italy and Jerusalem.

14 *The Bridge*. Pen and brown ink. Inscribed "IO SCO" with maker's mark in between. Probably drawn about 1524 on his return journey from Rome. On the reverse is a castle on rocks. The only drawing bearing this master's original signature.

PIETER AERTSZ, called LANGE PIER. B. Amsterdam, 1509; d. 1575. Active in Antwerp until 1555/56.

16 *The Adoration of the Shepherds*. Pen and brown ink and washes. Dated "1563." Preparatory sketch (vidimus) for a stained-glass window, intended to be submitted to the commissioner. After the latter's approval a full-size cartoon was made from the small design. Windows by Pieter Aertsz were probably once to be found in the Old Church in Amsterdam. None of these works, however, have been preserved.

DIRCK PIETERSZ CRABETH. B. Gouda (?), 1505; d. 1574. Worked in Gouda together with his younger brother Wouter (1520(?)-1589).

17 *Head of a Man*. Black chalk. The drawing was evidently connected with the making of a cartoon, but we know neither of any such cartoon, nor of the window for which it was designed. The drawing is related, however, to portraits on full-size cartoons intended for stained-glass windows preserved in Gouda that were made by the Crabeth brothers between 1555 and 1571.

DIRCK BARENDSZ. B. Amsterdam, 1534; d. 1592. Active in Venice for some years after 1555.

18 *Venetian Ball*. Pen with bluish-ink washes, heightened with white. Signed "Theodorus Bernardus (A)msterodamus Inventor" and dated "1574" on the shield. Engraved by Hendrick Goltzius in 1584. The customary title of the representation, *The Wedding of Antenor*, is based on a faulty interpretation of a hexameter (verse) that appears under the print: "Hic Antenorei Connubia magna Senatus . . ." Antenor, a hero from the Trojan Wars, was looked upon as the forefather of the Venetians. "Antenorei" here plainly refers to the descendants of Antenor, the Venetians. In the year 1574 the visit of Henry III of France was celebrated with a series of feasts.

CORNELIS KETEL. B. Gouda, 1548; d. Amsterdam, 1616. Active in London between 1573 and 1581.

19 *Corporation Piece*. Pen and brown ink and washes, heightened with white. Sketch for a lost painting of the year 1581 showing the civic guard under captain Herman Rodenborgh Bets.

HENDRICK GOLTZIUS. B. Mühlbracht, near Venlo, 1558; d. Haarlem, 1617.

20 *Christ Borne from the Tomb by Angels*. Engraved after a composition by Bartholomeus Spranger. Dated "A° 1587." Dedicated to Paul Sixt(us) Trautson, Lord High Chamberlain to Emperor Rudolf II. The Latin inscription was composed by the poet Franco van Est, a native of Gorinchem.

21 *Portrait of Giovanni da Bologna*. Black and red chalk, heightened with white. On the back a note by Goltzius: "Giovanni de Bolonia, Beelthouwer tot Florencen Geconterfeit. HG 1591" (HG ligature). When in Italy (1590-91), Goltzius made a series of these portraits of artists; examples are to be found, among others, in the Print Rooms in Amsterdam, Berlin, and Weimar, and in the collections of F. Lugt in Paris and of the late I. de Bruyn in Spiez.

22 *Study of a Tree*. Pen and brush in gray, brown, and green washes on blue paper. Inscribed with monogram "HG" (ligature). Drawn about 1600, during the period when Goltzius was changing over to painting.

25 *Landscape with Dunes near Haarlem*. Fine pen in

brown ink. Inscribed with monogram "HG" (ligature) and the date "1603" underneath the monogram of William Esdaile, the collector. The landscape as seen from one of the dunes, probably in the neighborhood of Bloemendaal.

ROELAND SAVERIJ. B. Courtrai, 1576; d. Utrecht, 1639. Besides in Utrecht, he worked in Amsterdam, Haarlem, Prague, Vienna, Salzburg, and Munich.

23 *Study of a Tree*. Chalk, oil pigments, and washes on brown paper. Signed "R. Sav." On the back "R. Savry" in red chalk.

JACOB DE GHEYN II. B. Antwerp, 1565: d. The Hague, 1629.

24 *Landscape with Highway Robbery*. Pen and brown ink on yellowish paper. Inscribed "JDGheyn in. 1603" (JDG ligature). In the South Netherlands particularly, in the first quarter of the seventeenth century, attacks by highwaymen were frequently depicted.

27 *Studies of a Fieldmouse*. Pen and brush and gray ink. Signed (later) "D: Geyn fec."

28 *Nude Studies*. Black chalk, pen and brown ink, heightened with white, on grayish paper. It has been suggested that the figures on this sheet were preparatory studies for a *Mary Magdalene*.

29 *Woman with Death*. Pen and brown ink. Inscribed "Jacques de Geijn 1600." Allegorical representation of vanity.

30 *Portrait of a Gentleman*. Leadpoint and red chalk on parchment. Made shortly before or around 1600. The sitter is unknown.

32 *Studies of Insects*. Pen and fine brush in different colored inks. Inscribed "DGheyn. fe. 1600" (DG ligature). Folio 11 from a little sketchbook with miniatures that once belonged to the Emperor Rudolf II of Hapsburg in Prague.

ABRAHAM BLOEMAERT. B. Gorinchem, 1564; d. Utrecht, 1651. Worked in Utrecht and also in France (Paris) and Amsterdam.

26 *Studies of Garden Plants*. Pen and gray ink, washes, and red chalk. On the back is a farmhouse. Page from a book of studies. Bloemaert frequently used realistic motifs of this sort in his compositions. He had already done a series of farmhouses before 1604.

BALTHASAR VAN DER AST. B. Middelburg, 1593 or 1594; d. Delft, 1657.

31 *Still Life with Fruit and Shells*. Pen and colored wash. Signed "B. vander. Ast . . ." Signed still lifes are fairly rare in the seventeenth century. The arrangement reproduced here was done about 1625 or later.

JAN VAN DE VELDE. B. Rotterdam (?), 1593; d. Enkhuizen, 1641.

33 *Fish Market*. Pen and brown ink, and washes, heightened with opaque white. Signed "J. V. Velde fecit." Van de Velde worked in Haarlem, Rotterdam, and Enkhuizen. The fish market does not appear to be identifiable, however.

CLAES JANSZ VISSCHER. B. Amsterdam, 1587; d. 1652.

34 *Loenersloot*. Pen and brown ink. About 1606/7 Claes Jansz drew a great number of such topographically identifiable landscapes, which he subsequently etched and issued as a series.

HENDRICK AVERKAMP. B. Amsterdam, 1585; d. Kampen, 1634.

35 *Winter Landscape*. Pen and ink, colored with water color. Inscribed with monogram "HA" (ligature) and later with "H A". The drawing was probably made at Kampen about 1625.

36 *Duck Hunter*. Pencil. It appears to have been drawn with a kind of graphite stylus, a material that came into

general use only later in the seventeenth century. In contrast with the previous drawing, this one has been done directly from life.

JAN ANTHONISZ VAN RAVESTEYN. B. The Hague, c. 1570; d. 1657.

37 *Civic Guard of the Company of St. Sebastian, The Hague.* Pen and brown ink, and washes, heightened with white on gray paper. Inscription by a later hand "de Baen." Preparatory sketch for the painting of 1618 in the Gemeentemuseum, The Hague, which represents *The Reception of the Civic Guard by the City Authorities in The Hague.*

GERARD TERBORGH THE ELDER. B. Zwolle, 1584; d. 1662. Between 1602 and 1612 travels through Germany, Italy, and France.

38 *The Tiber with the Ponte Rotto.* Pen and brown ink. Signed "G. T. Borch. F. in Roma. Anno. 16. ." In the Print Room in Amsterdam are more of such views of Rome, dated 1609.

THOMAS DE KEYSER. B. Amsterdam, 1596 or 1597; d. 1667.

39 *Civic Guard.* Pen and brown ink and wash. Made shortly after 1630. The painting for which this drawing served as compositional sketch is not known. The group in the middle recalls De Keyser's *Civic Guard of Captain Allaert Cloeck* (1632) in the Rijksmuseum, Amsterdam.

GERARD VAN HONTHORST. B. Utrecht, 1590; d. 1656. Lived in Italy between 1610 and 1621; later journeyed to England and Denmark.

40 *The Four Elements.* Pen and brown ink, and washes, heightened with white. Signed "Honthorst fecit." Drawn c. 1625 (?) No completely satisfactory explanation has yet been found for this representation in which the "Four Elements" and the "Four Seasons" have been combined.

WILLEM PIETERSZ BUYTEWEGH. B. Rotterdam, 1591 (?); d. 1624. Active also in Haarlem.

41 *Standing Cavalier.* Black chalk, heightened with white chalk, on gray paper. Inscribed with monogram "WB" (ligature). Later partly retouched. Drawn in 1622. There is a drawing intended as a pendant in the Ten Cate Collection in Almelo. The sheet was formerly kept in Dessau.

44 *Gunner and Camp Follower.* Etching, first state. Signed with monogram "WB" (ligature). Printed between 1615 and 1620.

47 *Trees by the Water.* Etching, second state (1621). Inscribed with monogram "WB" (ligature). Belongs to a group of landscape etchings made about 1616 (first state).

FRANS HALS. B. Antwerp or Malines, 1580 or 1581; d. Haarlem, 1666.

42 *Cavalier.* Black chalk, heightened with white, on gray paper. Made about 1625. Attributed to Frans Hals because of stylistic agreement with Civic Guard representations by his hand. Hitherto no authentic drawings by Frans Hals are known from this period.

WILLEM JACOBSZ DELFF. B. Delft, 1580; d. 1638.

43 *Cavalcade of the Princes of Nassau.* Engraving after a composition by Adriaen Pietersz van der Venne. Inscribed "W. Delff sculpsit I. P. Vennius exc. Middelb. 1621" and (below and right of center) "Adrianus Vennius Inventor." Those portrayed read, from left to right in the two front rows: Philip Willem, Prince Maurits, Prince Frederik Hendrik, Willem Lodewijk, Ernst Casimir and Johan Ernst. Adriaen van der Venne lived in The Hague.

JACOB DE GHEYN III. B. Amsterdam (?), 1596; d. Utrecht, 1641. Journeys to England, Sweden, and London.

45 *Sleeping Mars.* Etching, third state. Inscribed with monogram "IDG" (ligature) and "N. de Clerc exc. Hh" (Hh ligature). The representation is intended as an allegory on peace (while Mars is sleeping, the arts flourish).

ESAIAS VAN DE VELDE. B. Amsterdam, c. 1590; d. The Hague, 1630. Also active in Haarlem.

46 *Woods with Country Road.* Etching, first state. Inscribed "ESAIAS VAN DEN VELDE Fecit" and "I. P. Beerendrecht, excudit. Haerlemensis." Printed between 1620 and 1624.

HERCULES SEGHERS. B. Haarlem. c. 1590; d. Amsterdam (?), c. 1638. Also active in Utrecht and The Hague. Journeys to Brussels and also, possibly, south of the Alps.

48 *Two Trees with Fresh Foliage.* Etching, only copy known. Brown print on blue and reddish paper prepared with oil paint. Probably early work made about 1620 or earlier.

49 *Mossy Larch Tree.* Etching. Green-yellow print on orange-red and blue paper prepared with oil paint.

50 *Rocky Landscape with River.* Etching. Green print on light-green paper prepared with oil paint. Another copy (dark purple on a pink background) is in Leningrad.

51 *Still Life with Three Books.* Etching. Black print on canvas prepared with a gray ground. The background has been painted black. There is a second copy in the Albertina, Vienna. Prints of still lifes, for all practical purposes, are not encountered.

52 *The Great Tree.* Etching. Black print on white paper. A second copy was formerly in the Print Room in Dresden. The round building in the middle ground can also be seen in the painting in the Museum Boymans, Rotterdam. The dating (between 1620 and 1625?) must remain uncertain.

53 *Rocky Landscape with Four Trees.* Etching, first state. Black print on white paper. Other copies are to be found in Berlin (blue print on paper with a blue-white ground in oils) and in Dresden (black print on paper with a light-brown ground in oils).

GERARD TERBORGH THE YOUNGER. B. Zwolle, 1617; d. Deventer, 1681. Journeyed through England, Germany, France, Spain, and Italy. Active in Zwolle and Deventer and also in Haarlem.

54 *Haarlem Town Hall and Market.* Black chalk, pen and gray ink. Drawn during his apprenticeship years in Haarlem, between 1632 and 1635.

PIETER SAENREDAM. B. Assendelft, 1597; d. Haarlem, 1665. Chiefly active in Haarlem, but also from time to time in many other places in the Netherlands.

55 *Haarlem Market Place.* Pen and ink, with color washes. Inscribed "P. Saenredam. fecit. A°. 1629." The drawing was in the *album amicorum* of Petrus Scriverius, a native of Haarlem who was a professor of history at Leiden.

CORNELIS HENDRIKSZ VROOM. B. Haarlem, c. 1591; d. 1661.

56 *Forest Road.* Pen and brown ink, with pink and green washes. Drawn about 1630. Probably represented is the "Haerlems foreest" on the road to Leiden, poetically commemorated by Van Mander.

REMBRANDT. B. Leiden, 1606; d. Amsterdam, 1669.

57 *Portrait of the Artist's Father.* Red and black chalk, with brown washes. Seventeenth century (inscription by a later hand): "HARMAN GERRITS. van Rhijn." About 1630. On the back a sketch of a man sitting.

58 *Self Portrait.* Pen and brown ink, with gray washes, 1627 or 1628.

59 *Portrait of the Artist's Mother.* Pen and brush with

gray washes, 1628 or 1629. Drawn by candlelight. Related to an etching of 1628.

60 *Saskia with Child.* Pen and brown ink and washes. The sitter is usually considered to be Saskia, although this is not certain. The only one of Rembrandt's children not to die in infancy was Titus (b. 1641); the others all died before they were two months old. The date of 1636, hitherto generally agreed on, is probably too early.

61 *Hendrickje Stoffels.* Black chalk. Below right are collector's marks. Study for the painting, *Young Girl at the Window,* Dulwich, dated 1645. Hendrickje Stoffels' identity is purely conjectural.

62 *Christ Carrying the Cross.* Pen and brown ink and wash. Inscription by a later hand: "Rembrandt." About 1635.

63 *The Crucifixion.* Pen and brown ink, with brown washes. Some corrections in brown and white. About 1647.

64 *The Return of the Prodigal Son.* Pen and brown ink with brown washes. Corrections in white body color. Dated 1642 on an eighteenth-century etching after this drawing by I. J. de Claussin.

65 *View of the Singel at Amersfoort.* Pen and brown ink with brown washes. Below left and right are collectors' marks. In the distance, the houses in the Langestraat; left, the gardens of the houses of the Lievevrouwestraat. 1647 or 1648. Most of Rembrandt's landscapes originated in the surroundings of Amsterdam; there are some, however, from Rhenen and from the country round Haarlem.

66 *Two Farmhouses.* Reed pen and brown ink with brown washes. 1657 or 1658.

67 *Lioness Devouring a Bird.* Black chalk with gray washes, heightened with white on dark brown paper. About 1641.

68 *Oriental Horseman.* Pen and brown ink with brown and gray washes, red chalk, yellow water color, heightened with white on Chinese paper. Below, right, a collector's mark. Belongs to a series of drawings from Rembrandt's estate that were made after seventeenth-century miniatures by Hindustani artists. About 1654-56.

69 *Homer Reciting Poetry.* Reed pen and brown ink. Inscription in Rembrandt's own hand: "Rembrandt aen Joannes Sicx. 1652." The drawing is found in the "Pandora," the *album amicorum* of Jan Six.

70 *Female Nude from the Back.* Pen and brown ink, with brown washes. About 1658-61, Rembrandt made a large number of studies after the nude, this being one of them.

71 *Sleeping Young Woman (Hendrickje).* Brush and brown ink, 1655 or 1656. It is generally accepted that Hendrickje served as model here.

72 *Christ Raising Jairus's Daughter.* Pen and brown ink, with brown washes. About 1660-62. Representation taken from Matthew 9 : 23-26. On the reverse is the head of a young man, by another hand.

73 *Christ and the Woman Taken in Adultery.* Reed pen and brown ink, heightened with white body color. About 1659-60. Subject taken from John 8.

74 *Portrait of "Jan Six."* Reed pen and brown ink. About 1662. The sitter resembles both Titus and Jan Six. There exists stylistic agreement with sketches for *The Members of the Clothmakers Guild* as well as portraits of an even later date.

75 *Annunciation to the Shepherds.* Etching and graver, third state. Inscribed "Rembrandt f. 1634."

76 *The "Six" Bridge.* Etching, third state. Inscribed "Rembrandt f. 1645." According to a legend Rembrandt, during his stay at Six's country seat, wagered that he

could make an etching in the time required for a servant to fetch mustard, which had been forgotten, from the village nearby.

77 *The Hunter.* Etching and drypoint, first state. About 1652.

78 *"Hundred Guilder Print."* Etching, engraving and drypoint, second state on Japan paper. About 1649 or a little earlier. In this one composition Rembrandt has represented several moments from Christ's public life. They include *The Blessing of the Children, The Healing of the Sick,* and *The Rebuke given to the Rich Youth* (Matthew 19). The title was given to the etching during Rembrandt's own lifetime, when one print is said to have been sold for a hundred guilders.

79 *The Three Crosses.* Etching and drypoint, fourth state. Inscribed "Rembrandt f. 1653." The fourth state was reworked by Rembrandt in either 1660 or 1661.

80 *Reclining Nude.* Etching, drypoint and burin, second state. Inscribed "Rembrandt f. 1658." Known as *The Negress*; it is more likely to be a study made in the evening.

81 *Seated Nude.* Etching and drypoint, second state. Inscribed "Rembrandt f. 1658."

82 *Portrait of Dr. Arnold Tholinx.* Etching and drypoint, second state. Related to the portrait of Tholinx, made in 1656 in the Jacquemart-André Museum in Paris. The sitter was inspector of the College of Physicians of Amsterdam and brother-in-law of Jan Six.

FERDINAND BOL. B. Dordrecht, 1616; d. Amsterdam, 1680.

83 *Hagar in the Wilderness.* Pen and brown ink, with light-brown washes. First sketch for the painting in the Walker Art Gallery in Liverpool. Early work; the subject is taken from Genesis 16.

BAREND FABRITIUS. B. Middenbeemster, 1624; d. Amsterdam, 1673.

84 *Judas Returning the Pieces of Silver.* Pen and brush in brown and gray ink over black chalk, heightened with red chalk. Some corrections with white body color. On the reverse are old inscriptions: "Rembrandt" and "Judas." Subject taken from Matthew 27 : 3-7.

GERARD DOU. B. Leiden, 1613; d. 1675. Worked in Leiden and also, for a few years, in Amsterdam.

85 *An Old Man Cutting His Quill.* Black chalk. Signed (by a later hand?) "G. Dou." The background shows similarities to Rembrandt's early style of drawing.

GOVERT FLINK. B. Cleves, 1615; d. Amsterdam, 1660. Worked in Amsterdam and also in Leeuwarden.

86 *Studies of a Peacock.* Black and red chalk, brush and brown ink. About 1645-50, later used for the representation of peacocks in a painting (allegory on the birth of William III) done in 1650.

JACOB BACKER. B. Harlingen, 1608; d. Amsterdam, 1651. Worked in Amsterdam and also in Leeuwarden.

87 *Reclining Nude.* Black chalk, heightened with white on gray paper. Flinck, too, drew studies after the nude in this manner.

NICOLAES MAES. B. Dordrecht, 1632; d. Amsterdam, 1693.

88 *Girl with Basket.* Red chalk. Study for a painting, formerly in the Cook Collection at Richmond and dating from about 1655.

JAN LIEVENS. B. Leiden, 1607; d. Amsterdam, 1674. Spent some years in England (1632-34) and in Antwerp (between 1635 and 1644).

89 *Portrait of Gaspard Streso.* Black chalk. Inscribed with monogram "I. L." On the back is an eighteenth-century inscription: "Dominee Streso Predikant in 's-Gravenhage door J. Lievens na 't Leven getekent." Study for an

etching. Streso (1603-64) was a Calvinist minister in The Hague, where Lievens lived from 1654 till 1658.

93 *Forest Scene with Stag*. Pen and brown ink. Most of Lievens's forest scenes are presumed to have been done between 1650 and 1660. See also Plate IV.

GERBRANDT VAN DEN EECKHOUT. B. Amsterdam, 1621; d. 1674.

90 *Boy Sitting on a Chair*. Brush and brown ink, heightened with white. Late work, style anticipating eighteenth-century developments. The sheet used to be considered the work of Fragonard, who is known to have made similar studies. Van den Eeckhout carried out many studies in this brush technique.

LAMBERT DOOMER. B. Amsterdam, 1622 or 1623; d. Alkmaar, 1700. Journeyed through France, Germany, and England.

91 *The Castle at Saumur*. Pen and gray ink, with brown wash. Made in the summer of 1646 on one of the artist's trips with Willem Schellinks along the Loire.

ANTHONIE VAN BORSSUM. B. Amsterdam, 1629 (?); d. 1677.

92 *Windmill and Rolling Bridge*. Pen and brown ink on black chalk, with gray, brown, and pink water-color washes. Signed "AVBorssum" (AVB ligature).

ABRAHAM FURNERIUS. B. Amsterdam (?) 1628; d. Rotterdam, 1654.

94 *Forest Scene with Road*. Pen and brush in brown ink over red chalk. Furnerius was a pupil of Rembrandt after 1645 and a son-in-law of Philips Koninck.

ADRIAEN VAN OSTADE. B. Haarlem, 1610; d. 1684.

95 *Study for a Family Group Portrait*. Pen and brown ink over pencil, with gray washes. One of three studies for the family group in the Louvre painted in 1654. It can be seen from the painting that Van Ostade made further changes in the composition after this sketch had been made. Considered by some to be the artist's own family.

96 *Backgammon Players*. Pen and light brown ink, with gray washes.

ISAAC VAN OSTADE. B. Haarlem, 1621; d. 1649.

97 *Adoration of the Shepherds*. Pen and brush in brown ink over pencil. Inscribed "I. v. Ost . ." Below right is a collector's mark.

JAN HAVICKSZ STEEN. B. Leiden, 1626; d. 1679. Worked in Leiden and also in The Hague, Delft, Warmond, and Haarlem.

98 *Gay Company in an Arbor*. Pen and brown ink, brush in brown and gray ink on black chalk. Study for a painting now in the Boston Museum.

JAN VAN GOYEN. B. Leiden, 1596; d. The Hague, 1656. Also active in Haarlem. Journeyed through Belgium, Germany, France, and made trips in Holland.

99 *Landscape with a Windmill*. Black chalk. Inscribed "VG 1644" (VG ligature).

ALBERT CUYP. B. Dordrecht, 1620; d. 1691.

100 *Landscape with River and Cows*. Black chalk and brown washes. Probably a picture of the Meuse near Dordrecht.

104 *Wooded Landscape*. Black chalk with green-brown and blue washes. This drawing is considered to be an early work, made about 1650.

AERT VAN DER NEER. B. Amsterdam, 1603; d. 1677.

101 *Landscape with Three Farmhouses*. Brush and brown ink. Only a few drawings by Aert van der Neer are known and they are all in this style.

JAN VAN DE CAPPELLE. B. Amsterdam, 1626; d. 1679.

102 *Golf-playing on the Ice*. Brush and gray ink.

PHILIPS KONINCK. B. Amsterdam, 1619; d. 1688. Also worked in Rotterdam.

103 *Distant View with River*. Pen and brown and gray ink.

Inscribed on the back "P. Koning." There is a preparatory sketch for this drawing in the museum at Rennes.

JACOB ISAACKSZ VAN RUISDAEL. B. Haarlem, 1629; d. Amsterdam (probably), 1682. Journeys to France and through Western Germany.

105 *Forest Scene*. Etching, first state. Inscribed "JvRuysdael f." (JvR ligature). Publisher's mark "F. v. W. excud." Early work, made about 1648.

106 *Grainfield*. Etching, fourth state. Inscribed "JvRuysdael fe." (JvR ligature).

107 *Interior of the Old Church, Amsterdam*. Black chalk and pencil, with gray wash. Old inscription "d'oude Kerk," over which has been written in different ink "J. Ruisdael." Left of this is a collector's mark. This drawing and that of the interior of the New Church in Amsterdam which is preserved in the Print Room in Berlin are exceptions in the œuvre of this landscape painter. Apart from the many signed church interiors by Pieter Saenredam there are few other known seventeenth-century examples of this genre.

108 *View of a Beach*. Black chalk and gray wash, heightened with white on grayish paper. Probably the beach near Zandvoort.

ALLAERT VAN EVERDINGEN. B. Alkmaar, 1621; d. Amsterdam, 1675. Also active in Utrecht and Haarlem. Journeyed to Sweden.

109 *Mountain Landscape in Sweden*. Brush and gray ink on gray paper. Between 1640 and 1644 the artist was commissioned by Mr. Trip to visit his gun foundry at Julitabroeck (Södermanland) in Sweden. He returned with a large number of travel sketches.

112 *Coastal Landscape with Rocks*. Etching, first state. Inscribed with monogram "AVE." None of Van Everdingen's etchings are dated.

REINIER NOOMS, called ZEEMAN. B. Amsterdam (?) c. 1623; d. before April 1667. Worked in Amsterdam. Journeys to France (Paris), London, sea voyage to North Africa.

110 *The Element of Air*. Etching, first state. Signed ".R. Seeman. In &. f." Inscription "LAIR." This and No. 111 are from a series of the Four Elements.

111 *The Element of Water*. Etching, first state. Inscription "L'EAU." See No. 110.

MEINDERT HOBBEMA. B. Amsterdam, 1638; d. 1709.

113 *Church and Watermill at Deventer*. Black chalk and wash. Preparatory study for a painting. Made about 1660.

PAULUS POTTER. B. Enkhuizen, 1625; d. Amsterdam, 1654. Worked in Amsterdam and also in Haarlem, Delft, and The Hague.

114 *Deer in a Wood*. Black chalk. Inscribed "P. Potter f. 1647."

BARTHOLOMEUS VAN DER HELST. B. Haarlem, 1613; d. Amsterdam, 1670.

115 *Man Seated*. Black and white chalk on gray paper. Study for undated painting in the Hermitage, Leningrad. The costume would suggest it to have been drawn sometime between 1653 and 1655.

ANTHONIE WATERLOO. B. Lille, 1609 or 1610; d. Utrecht, 1676 or later. Worked in Utrecht and also in Amsterdam, Leeuwarden, and in places along the River Vecht. Journeyed to Germany and Italy.

116 *Oude Gracht in Utrecht*. Black chalk and gray washes. Inscribed "A. Waterloo." The Oude Gracht, a canal in Utrecht, near the Smeerbrug.

ROELAND ROGHMAN. B. Amsterdam, 1597; d. 1686.

117 *The Castle at Wijk bij Duurstede*. Black chalk with gray washes. Signed "R. Roghman." The artist developed a

repertory of 247 castles in the Netherlands, this drawing being one of them. The commissioner of the series is unknown; it is known that the series was executed during 1646 and 1647 and formed part of Hillebrand Bentes's estate in 1708. The drawings remained together till 1800.

GABRIËL METSU. B. Leiden, 1629; d. Amsterdam, 1667.
118 *Woman with a Silver Basin.* Black chalk, heightened with white on gray paper. Wrongly inscribed "T. Bor . ." (Gerard Terborch). Study for the woman in a painting formerly in the Rothschild Collection at Frankfort.

ADRIAEN VAN DE VELDE. B. Amsterdam, 1636; d. 1672.
119 *Two Country Girls.* Red chalk. Signed "Adrianus v.d. Velde fe." Sheet of studies. The hands of the girl in front have been drawn again separately.

JAN DE BRAY. B. Haarlem, c. 1627; d. 1697.
120 *Portrait of a Girl.* Inscribed "JDBray" (JDB ligature) and "1663."

CORNELIS VISSCHER. B. Haarlem, 1629; d. Amsterdam, 1662.
121 *Head of a Boy.* Chalk on parchment. Most of this artist's portrait drawings were between 1652 and 1658. C. Visscher's work as an engraver was not inconsiderable and he left 185 prints on his death.

CASPAR NETSCHER. B. Heidelberg, 1639; d. The Hague, 1684.
122 *Girl with a Top.* Black chalk. Probably an early work (about 1665).
123 *Young Woman at a Window.* Pen and brown ink and wash. Inscribed "C.Netscher" (C and N ligature). Preparatory study for a painting.

BARTHOLOMEUS BREENBERGH. B. Deventer, 1599 or 1600; d. Amsterdam, before March 1659.
124 *View of Tivoli.* Pen and brown ink and wash. Inscribed "B. Breenbergh f. Roma An° 1625" and "BB f." In a later hand "a Tivoli." The artist lived in Rome from 1620 until 1629. He preferred to draw Italianate landscapes with classical ruins.

JAN BOTH. B. Utrecht, c. 1610; d. 1652.
125 *View in the Campagna Showing the Tiber.* Etching. Inscribed "J. Both fc." Made after Both's sojourn in Rome (1636-40) where he had come under the influence of, among others, Claude Lorrain, the landscape painter.

CLAES PIETERSZ (NICOLAES) BERCHEM. B. Haarlem, 1620; d. Amsterdam, 1683.
126 *Man Riding a Mule.* Etching, second state. Inscribed "Berghem 1644." Printed during his stay in Italy (1642-45). Of his many pastoral scenes this early etching was honored with the name of "the pearl" on account of its unprecedented handling of light.

JAN DE BISSCHOP (MAGISTER JOHANNUS EPISCOPIUS). B. Amsterdam, 1628; d. The Hague, 1671. He not only drew topographical views but also copied old masters.
127 *Two Persons Sketching at Zorgvliet, The Hague.* Pen and brown ink with washes prepared by the artist himself from rusty nails and later called "bishop's ink" from the name of its originator. The sketchers are sitting at the entrance to the country seat known as Zorgvliet on the Oude Scheveningse Weg, the road from The Hague to Scheveningen.

VALENTIJN KLOTZ. Active in Brabant and Limburg between 1669 and 1697.
128 *View of Maastricht.* Pen and brown ink with colored washes. Inscribed "tot Maestricht geteeckent den i Maeij Anno 1671." We know of numerous topographical drawings in the south of Holland made by Klotz, who was a draughtsman and engineer. Carefully dated, they

deal for the most part with the campaigns of William III against Louis XIV.

JAN VAN DER HEYDEN. B. Gorinchem, 1637; d. Amsterdam, 1712.
129 *Firemen at a Fire.* Pen and gray washes. About 1690. Design for an "advertisement" that was never carried out. In the top left-hand corner is a fire engine and, beside it, Minerva with a torch. Van der Heyden showed great technical interest in the improvement of the techniques of fire fighting: several inventions in this field are credited to his name. In 1690 appeared the first edition of his richly illustrated *Brandspuitenboek* (Book of Fire Engines).

CONSTANTIJN HUYGENS THE YOUNGER. B. The Hague, 1628; d. 1697. Secretary to William III.
130 *View of The Hague.* Pen and brush and reddish-brown ink. Dated on the back "18 Sept. 1666." The drawing was for a long time ascribed to J. Lingelbach.

WILLEM VAN DE VELDE THE YOUNGER. B. Leiden, 1633; d. London, 1707. He settled in London in 1673.
131 *The IJ at Amsterdam.* Pen with brown and gray washes.
132 *Ship.* Pen and brown washes.

LUDOLF BACKHUYZEN. B. Emden, 1631; d. Amsterdam, 1708.
133 *The Man-of-War* King William *off Rotterdam.* Pen and brown wash. Study for the painting dated "1689" in the Rijksmuseum, Amsterdam.
134 *Returning Seafarers.* Pen and brown washes. Late work.

CORNELIS SAFTLEVEN. B. Gorinchem, c. 1607; d. Rotterdam, 1681.
135 *Raccoons.* Black chalk with color washes. Inscribed with monogram.

ALBERT VAN DEN EECKHOUT. Worked in Brazil from 1637 till 1644 as court painter to Johan Maurits of Nassau; lived for many years in Amersfoort; worked in Saxony from 1655 till about 1663 at the elector's court; subsequently, possibly, in Groningen, where a certain "Albert Eckholt, painter" is mentioned in 1664.
136 *Brazilian Owl.* Chalk and brush drawing. Study from life. This and many other studies of plants and animals made by him in Brazil were destroyed by fire in Berlin during the Second World War.

HERMAN SAFTLEVEN. B. Rotterdam, 1610; d. Utrecht, 1685.
137 *Cactus.* Pen and color washes. Inscribed "HS f. 1683. den. 20. Septer." (HS ligature). Mentioned among the drawings acquired by Valerius Röver (1686-1739) from the estate of Agnes Block (1629-1704).

MARIA SIBYLLE MERIAN. B. Frankfort, 1647; d. Amsterdam, 1717. She lived, from 1684 onward, as a devotee of Jean de Labadie at the Labadists' Colony "Waltahuis" (at Wiewerd, Friesland). She owned a collection of exotic insects sent to her from Surinam (Netherlands West Indies). She visited Surinam herself around 1700.
138 *Study of Plant and Insects.* Water color. Inscribed "M.S. Merian." Inscribed on the back "Een Spinne die een Vogel uytsuygt en in syn poten gevadt heeft rode klaeuwen, 1 Sprinckhaen of Levendig bladt, Chrysanthemum Africanum alata Caule de Vera Crus. annua." (A spider sucking a bird dry, its legs grasping red claws; a grasshopper or praying mantis; Chrysanthemum Africanum alata Caule de Vera Crus, annua.) Drawn about 1696.

AERT SCHOUMAN. B. Dordrecht, 1710; d. The Hague, 1792. Was president of the art academy in The Hague from 1752 to 1762 and president of the confraternity Pictura, 1777-92.
139 *Two Crested Peacocks.* Water color. Inscription on the

back: "Twee pauwisen levensgroot zijnde als een kalckoen A. d. 1754." (Two peacocks as large as turkeys ...) One of the earliest Netherlandish examples of pure water color.

JAN LUYKEN. B. Amsterdam, 1649; d. 1712.

140 *Herod Making War on the Robbers.* Pen and gray washes. Preparatory study for the print of 1704 which served as an illustration to *Flavius Josephus, alle de Werken, Behelzende Twintig Boeken van de Joodsche Oudheden, 't Verhaal van zijn eygen Leeven, De Histori van de Oorlogen der Jooden tegens de Romeynen enz... in 't Nederduytsche overgebragt door W. Sewel – by Pieter Mortier, Boekverkoper MDCCIV t'Amsterdam.*

JOHANNES GLAUBER, called POLYDOOR. B. Utrecht, 1646; d. Schoonhoven, c. 1726.

141 *Mountain Landscape.* Pen-and-ink drawing. The artist lived in Italy from 1674 to 1679, during which period this drawing must have been executed. An example of pure pen-and-ink drawing, after the Italian manner.

JACOB DE WIT. B. Amsterdam, 1696; d. 1754.

142 *Design for a Ceiling.* Pen and gray ink with brown wash. Inscribed "J. de Wit invt." Drawn in 1746. Annotated on the back: "Plaffon geschildert voor mejuffrouw de Wede. A. B. Barnards. Hoekstuck voor mejuffrouw de Wede. A. B. Barnards 1746 te Haarlem." (Ceiling painted for Miss de Wede. A. B. Barnards. Cornerpiece for Miss de Wede. A. B. Barnards, 1746, at Haarlem.) The ceiling represents the Apotheosis of Hercules. The four spandrels show: *Hercules Capturing the Erymanthean Boar; The Slaying of the Hydra; Hercules Slaying the Nemean Lion; Hercules Capturing the Cretan Bull.*

CORNELIS TROOST. B. Amsterdam, 1697; d. 1750.

143 *A Reception.* Pen and brown ink and wash. Rough sketch for a composition. The faces of the persons attending a reception in a Louis XV interior are indicated by an oval and cross.

145 *Portrait of a Girl.* Pastel and body color. The drawing, which has more the character of a sketch, has been carried out in a technique used by Troost repeatedly: a combination of pastel and body color.

HENDRIK POTHOVEN. B. Amsterdam, 1728; d. The Hague, 1793.

144 *Child in High Chair.* Black chalk, heightened with white on blue-gray paper. First study of child of the family of Jacob Swarth for a group portrait made in 1775 which is in the possession of the F. G. Insinger family. A study for the eldest daughter in this family portrait is preserved in the A. Staring Collection. A third study is owned by the Museum Boymans, Rotterdam.

JAN VAN HUYSUM. B. Amsterdam, 1682; d. 1749.

146 *Study of Plants and Flowers.* Water color over oiled charcoal. Signed and dated "1731."

JACOB CATS. B. Altona, 1741; d. Amsterdam, 1799. Drew amateur copies after old masters.

147 *View from the Tafelberg.* Pen and water color. Belongs to a series of four views in Gooiland: "In an extensive prospect can be seen Laaren Churchyard, Cooltjes or Tafelberg, Huyzen, Blarikom, Laaren, Kneckelbak and Eemnes Buiten" (description in the auction catalogue of the Amsterdam burgomaster P. C. Hasselaar, 1797, for whom the drawings were made). Cats's numerous topographical drawings were usually done from memory and are not very reliable.

REINIER VINKELES. B. Amsterdam, 1741; d. 1816. Was secretary of the Art Academy ("Stads-Teekenacademie") from 1762 onward. Stayed in Paris from 1770 to 1771.

148 *Winter Scene on the Buiten-Amstel near the Beerebijt.* Chalk and brush. Inscribed "R. Vinkeles ad vivum f. 1769." The drawing is in the *Atlas Splitgerber* (1872, No. 281) of the Municipality of Amsterdam, which contains a large number of topographical subjects.

DIRK LANGENDIJK. B. Rotterdam, 1748; d. 1805.

149 *The Fire in the St. John's Church, Arnhem.* Pen and brown ink, and wash. The drawing was made to commemorate the plundering of Arnhem by French soldiers in 1795. Another drawing treating the same subject and dated "1795" is in the H. van Leeuwen Collection.

WYBRAND HENDRIKS. B. Amsterdam, 1744; d. Haarlem, 1831. President of the Haarlem Art Academy ("Teekenacademie") and from 1786 to 1819 "castellan" of Teyler's Foundation and superintendent of the art collection. He made drawings after old masters for Collectors.

150 *Maples under the Snow in the Haarlem Woods.* Chalk and water color. A drawing related in subject and technique is to be found in the Museum Fodor, Amsterdam, and is dated "1820."

SIMON FOKKE. B. Amsterdam, 1712; d. 1784.

151 *The Utrecht Towboat.* Pen, brush, and gray wash.

JACOBUS PERKOIS. B. Middelburg, 1756; d. 1804. Joint founder of and teacher at the Art School in Middelburg in 1778.

152 *Three Figures.* Red and black chalk and water color. These vivid sketches of folk characters done in red and black chalk with the aid of water color are characteristic of Perkois as a draughtsman. Many of them appeared as engravings in M. de Sallieth's *Verzameling van verschillende gekleurde mans- en vrouwenstanden,* Rotterdam, 1818.

CHARLES HOWARD HODGES. B. Portsmouth, 1764; d. Amsterdam, 1837. Worked in Amsterdam and The Hague and also for many years in London.

153 *Two Ladies Making Music.* Black and red chalk with brush and gray ink on blue paper. Dated "A° 1806." Undoubtedly done in Holland.

PAULUS VAN LIENDER. B. Utrecht, 1731; d. 1797. Was committee member of the Haarlem Art Academy ("Stads-Teekenacademie").

154 *Forest Scene.* Pen and brown ink and wash.

JACOB VAN STRIJ. B. Dordrecht, 1756; d. 1815.

155 *Summer Scene outside Dordrecht.* Brush and gray and brown ink. Study for the painting in the Dordrecht Museum, made c. 1800. In this and in many of his other works the artist has been inspired by Anthonie van Borssum and his seventeenth-century fellow-townsman Albert Cuyp.

BAREND CORNELIS KOEKKOEK. B. Middelburg, 1803; d. Cleves, 1862. Moved to Cleves in 1836, where he founded the art school in 1841.

156 *Study of Trees.* Water color. Early work, probably done before 1836 during the time when he was working on the edge of the Veluwe, near Wolfheze, and in Beek, near Nijmegen.

JURRIAEN ANDRIESSEN. B. Amsterdam, 1742; d. 1819. Was vice president of the "Stads-Teekenacademie" from 1794 till his death. In 1805 he founded an academy in his own house, where students specialized in "the study of the coloring of the female body in the nude."

157 *The Camera Obscura.* Pen and brown ink and washes. Inscribed "20 July" and "La Chambre obscure." Late work. Drawing with the aid of a camera obscura had come into use at the beginning of the seventeenth century or earlier. In the eighteenth century Canaletto (Venice), among others, had drawn cityscapes with its

help, and at the beginning of the nineteenth century it was once more extremely popular.

WOUTER JOHANNES VAN TROOSTWIJK. B. Amsterdam, 1782; d. 1810.

158 *Man Seated.* Pen and brown ink and wash. Inscribed "vTroostwijk 1808."

DAVID PIERRE HUMBERT DE SUPERVILLE. B. The Hague, 1770; d. Leiden, 1849. In 1795 he was given the sobriquet "Giottino" by his Roman friends and in 1816 he had it added to his name legally, in the form of "Giottin." From 1814 to 1823 director of the Leiden art school and, from 1825 until his death, director of the Leiden Print Room. One of the earliest lithographers in Holland.

159 *The Flood.* Water color. Numerous detail studies for this drawing in either chalk or pencil have been preserved, all of them in the Leiden Print Room, where there are almost a hundred other drawings by this artist as well as some etchings and lithographs. Among other remarks Humbert has this to say on the subject (the Flood): "Of the last of the earth's giants or tyrants... no more is visible than his legs hanging over a... tree that has collapsed under the burden of sin... and his Crown, symbol of dominion, rolls... A Serpent, symbol of sin... spits its venom at its companion in evil by way of parting greeting. The comet, now our moon, is seen covered with bloodstains... while the Ark drifts gently over the wide waters." The colors which he used for this and similar realistic visions vary between violet-pink, green-yellow, brown, and, above all, dark blue.

160 *Ice Floes on the Meuse.* Chalk and brush in gray ink. Inscribed "glaçons sur la Meuse, Janvier 1809" and "G. Humbert d'après nature." Representations of actual landscapes are exceptional in Humbert's œuvre. Our example shows the piling up and grinding together of floes as the ice breaks up on the Meuse.

SIMON ANDREAS KRAUSZ. B. The Hague, 1760; d. 1825.

161 *Head of a Calf.* Colored chalk, pen and brown ink. Inscribed "S. A. Krausz f."

ABRAHAM VAN STRIJ. B. Dordrecht, 1753; d. 1826. One of the founders of the draughtsmen's confraternity called Pictura at Dordrecht in 1774. In his interiors he imitated Pieter de Hoogh and Gabriël Metsu, among others, and in his landscapes Albert Cuyp.

162 *The Connoisseur.* Pen and gray and brown ink and washes. About 1820.

WIJNAND JAN JOSEPH NUYEN. B. The Hague, 1813; d. 1839.

163 *Rue du Gros-Horloge, Rouen.* Water color in brown. Inscribed "W. J. J. Nuyen." Probably made about 1833 during one of his journeys through Belgium and France.

JOHANNES BOSBOOM. B. The Hague, 1817; d. 1891.

164 *Interior of the Geertekerk, Utrecht.* Water color. Made between 1840 and 1850. The artist was especially famous for his numerous sepia drawings and his water colors of church interiors, in which he was clearly inspired by the Dutch masters of the seventeenth century.

CHARLES ROCHUSSEN. B. Kralingen (Rotterdam), 1814; d. Rotterdam, 1894. Acquired a name as a book illustrator as well as a painter of historical and military scenes.

165 *Outpost of the Hussars.* Water color. Inscribed "CR f.73."

WILLEM MARIS. B. The Hague, 1844; d. 1910. The youngest of the three Maris brothers.

166 *Girl Herding Cows.* Water color. Inscribed "W. Maris fe." An example of a drawing from his early period when he was still under the influence of Matthijs. Made about 1865.

MATTHIJS (THIJS) MARIS. B. The Hague, 1839; d. London, 1917.

167 *The Royal Children.* Charcoal. Inscribed "MM." Maris also represented the romance of the two "royal children" in a painting. The artist shows himself strongly influenced by German Romantic painting and literature of the early nineteenth century. Probably drawn in Paris between 1872 and 1875.

AUGUST(US) ALLEBÉ. B. Amsterdam, 1838; d. 1927. From 1870 onward was professor and later also head of the "Rijksacademie."

168 *Portrait of Aunt Thérèse.* Pencil, face in water color. Inscribed "August Allebé Sept 28.58."

PAUL JOSEPH CONSTANTIN GABRIËL. B. Amsterdam, 1828; d. Scheveningen, 1903.

169 *Farmyard.* Black chalk. Inscribed "Gabriel." A landscape in Gelderland, drawn between 1860 and 1870.

JACOBUS HENDRICUS (JACOB) MARIS. B. The Hague, 1837; d. Karlsbad, 1899.

170 *The Schreierstoren, Amsterdam.* Charcoal. Inscribed "J. Maris." This subject returns in various paintings by Jacob Maris.

WILLEM ROELOFS. B. Amsterdam, 1822; d. Berchem (near Antwerp), 1897.

171 *Landscape.* Black chalk.

ANTON MAUVE. B. Zaandam, 1838; d. Arnhem, 1888.

172 *The Sale of Timber.* Water color. Inscribed "A. Mauve."

JOHANNES HENDRIK WEISSENBRUCH. B. The Hague, 1824; d. 1903. Did landscapes in water color mainly and must not be confused with his elder brother Johannes (Jan), who was a painter of town views.

173 *Polder Landscape.* Water color. Inscribed "J. H. Weissenbruch."

JOHAN BARTHOLD JONGKIND. B. Lattrop (Overijsel), 1819; d. Côte-Saint-André (near Grenoble), 1891.

174 *The Jazon at Rotterdam.* Water color. Inscribed on the back "de Jason 30 Septemb. 56 Rotterdam." Drawn during his stay in Rotterdam from 1855 to 1860.

175 *The Quays of the Seine in Paris.* Water color in yellow and blue over pencil sketch. Made in 1862 or 1863.

176 *The Seine near Bas-Meudon.* Water color. Inscribed "Meudon 29/4 1866 Sèvres Jongkind."

177 *View of Grenoble.* Water color and black chalk. Inscribed "Jongkind 1877" and "Grenoble" and, on the back, "16 September 1877."

178 *La Côte Saint-André.* Water color and black chalk. Inscribed "la Côte 2 mars 1885 Jongkind." On the back is a sketch of a country road. Jongkind stayed at Côte-Saint-André from 1878 onward.

GEORGE HENDRIK BREITNER. B. Rotterdam, 1857; d. Amsterdam, 1923.

179 *Galloping Horse Artillery.* Water color. Inscribed "G. H. Breitner." Drawn about 1887.

180 *Saturday Evening Market in the Rain on the Prinsegracht, The Hague.* Water color. Inscribed "G. H. Breitner." Drawn about 1882.

181 *Reclining Nude.* Black chalk. Inscribed "G. H. Breitner." Drawn between 1892 and 1895. Preparatory study for the painting of a reclining nude which is in the Gemeentemuseum, The Hague.

182 *Pile Driving near the IJ, Amsterdam.* Black chalk and pastels. Inscribed "G. H. Breitner '97." Preparatory study for the painting dated "1897" in the Stedelijk Museum, Amsterdam. The ideas for many of Breitner's paintings from these years came to him during his wanderings in the neighborhood of his new studio, which was built in 1897 on the Prinseneiland at the IJ.

JOZEF ISRAËLS. B. Groningen, 1824; d. The Hague, 1911.

183 *Woman Drinking Coffee.* Black chalk. Inscribed "Jozef Israels." Drawn about 1900.

SUZE BISSCHOP-ROBERTSON. B. The Hague, 1856; d. 1922.
184 *Boy Sitting on a Bench.* Black chalk. Inscribed "Suze Robertson." Probably drawn around 1900.

MARIUS ALEXANDER JACQUES BAUER, called RUSTICUS. B. The Hague, 1864; d. Amsterdam, 1932. Made many extensive journeys, among others to the Far East.
185 *The Horses of San Marco, Venice.* Black chalk and wash. Inscribed with monogram "MB." Drawn in 1895. The drawing is of the four Late Greek horses in gilded copper that the Venetians took as booty from Constantinople in 1204.

WILHELMUS HENDRICUS PETRUS JOHANNES (WILLEM) DE ZWART. B. The Hague, 1862; d. 1931.
186 *Girl Reading.* Black and colored chalk. Inscribed "W. de Z."

ISAÄC (LAZARUS) ISRAËLS. B. Amsterdam, 1865; d. The Hague, 1934. Son of Jozef Israëls.
187 *Lady with Cigarette, Reading.* Water color with a little chalk. Inscribed "Isaac Israels." Made about 1895.

VINCENT WILLEM VAN GOGH. B. Groot-Zundert, 1853; d. Auvers-sur-Oise, 1890.
188 *Mother and Child.* Charcoal and pencil, heightened with white, with brown wash. Inscribed "Vincent." Drawn in 1882 during his stay in The Hague (1881-83). The sitters are Sien and her daughter.
189 *The Gravedigger.* Charcoal. Drawn in 1885 during his stay at home in Nuenen (1883-85).
190 *Behind the Schenkweg, The Hague.* Pen and brush, pencil, heightened with white. Inscribed "Vincent. fe." Drawn in May 1882. View from the window of his studio at the Schenkweg in The Hague. Belongs to the second series of (seven) town views that Vincent made on commission from his uncle. He drew this view repeatedly, first in January 1882.
191 *Landscape at Nuenen.* Pen and ink, heightened with white. Inscribed "Vincent." Drawn at Nuenen in May 1884.
192 *The Grote Markt at Antwerp.* Black chalk and red and blue pencil, on bluish paper. Drawn on December 18, 1885, during Van Gogh's three months' stay in Antwerp. The drawing shows the Great Market in Antwerp, with the Winkler house and the Cathedral.
193 *Dead Sparrows.* Black chalk. Drawn in Antwerp, in February 1886. The drawing is on the reverse of a sheet whose obverse shows seven studies of hands.
194 *Summerhouse with Sunflower.* Pen and water color. Drawn in 1887 during his stay in Paris (1886-88).
195 *Peasant from the Camargue.* Pen and brush in gray ink. Signed "Vincent." Drawn in August 1888 during his stay at Arles (1888-89).
196 *La Crau.* Pen, reed pen, and black chalk. Signed "Vincent. La Crau, vue prise à Montmajor." Made in May 1888 in the neighborhood of Arles.
197 *The Rock.* Reed pen and gray ink with traces of pencil. Signed "Vincent." Made in July 1888 at Arles.
198 *Saint-Rémy under a Starry Sky.* Pen and brush, and gray ink. Made in 1889 or 1890 at Saint-Rémy. The drawing was lost in the Second World War.
199 *Plumed Hyacinth.* Reed pen and pencil. Drawn at Saint-Rémy in 1890.
200 *Peasants at Their Meal.* Black chalk and pencil. Drawn in 1889 or 1890 at Saint-Rémy.
201 *Town Hall, Auvers.* Black chalk. Drawn in 1890 at Auvers, where Van Gogh spent the last two months of his life.

ANTONIUS JOHANNES (ANTOON) DERKINDEREN. B. 's-Hertogenbosch, 1859; d. Amsterdam 1925.

202 *Portrait of Chaplain C. J. Tholenaer.* Pencil sketch for the *Procession of the Miraculous Holy Sacrament,* painted in 1888 and now in the Begijnhof, Amsterdam. In all, there are more than 70 preparatory studies in the Begijnhof, most of them in chalk, some in pencil, charcoal, and ink.

HENDRIK JOHANNES HAVERMAN. B. Amsterdam, 1858; d. The Hague, 1928.
203 *Portrait of Dr. Johannes Hendrik Caspar Kern.* Black chalk, heightened with white. Signed "Haverman 1896." Dr. Kern (1833-1917) was professor of Sanskrit, Indian Archeology, and Comparative Philology at Leiden.

WILLEM ARNOLDUS WITSEN. B. Amsterdam, 1860; d. 1923.
204 *Portrait of Jacobus van Looy.* Red and black chalk. Signed "W.W." and "Amsterdam September 1891." The writer-poet Jacobus van Looy (1855-1930), one of the most typical of the "Tachtigers" (the artistic generation of the 1880s), was himself an accomplished painter and draughtsman. His work is still, for the most part, preserved in the Jacob van Looy Museum in Haarlem.

JAN PIETER VETH. B. Dordrecht, 1864; d. Amsterdam, 1925. Professor at the "Rijksacademie."
205 *Portrait of Dr. Abraham Kuyper.* Black chalk. Veth made the studies for his portrait of this influential theologian and politician (1837-1920) during Kuyper's lectures at the Free University in Amsterdam. Signed "JV" (ligature). Drawing for the lithograph of 1892 in the *Amsterdammer* of 17th January. Veth painted his portrait in oils in 1897.

JAN THEODOOR TOOROP. B. Purworedjo (Java), 1858; d. The Hague, 1928.
206 *Garden of Sorrows.* Black chalk. Inscribed on stone "Jan Toorop." Drawn in 1890 or early 1891, the years in which his first Symbolist works appeared. The whereabouts of the drawing are unknown since 1911.
207 *"O Grave, Where Is Thy Victory?"* Black chalk on yellow cardboard. Signed "Jan Toorop '92." The title has been taken from the King James Version, which properly reads: "O death, where is thy victory? O death, where is thy sting?" (I Corinthians 15 : 55). The figures at the right are Envy, Spite, Jealousy, Hate, Love, and Strife. Above the dying hover two seraphim who remove the thorns from their bodies, thereby indicating the end of earthly suffering and the beginning of the redemption of the soul.
208 *The Apostles Thomas and Thaddeus.* Black chalk. Inscribed "Jth. Toorop Nijmegen 1909." The drawing is one of a series of the Apostles intended for a wall painting that was never executed. Best known are: *Andrew and James* (1910), *Peter* (1910), *Paul* (1911), and *Bartholomew* (1912).

RICHARD NICOLAUS ROLAND HOLST. B. Amsterdam, 1868; d. 1938. A professor at the "Rijksacademie" from 1918 and also director from 1926 onward.
209 *Preaching in the Fields.* Black chalk and color. Inscribed "R. N. Roland Holst 1892." We learn from Holst's correspondence with Toorop that the drawing was made in March.

FLORIS VERSTER. B. Leiden, 1861; d. 1927.
210 *Endegeest.* Wax crayon and water color. The drawing represents part of the Endegeest Park in Leiden. Signed "Floris Verster." Drawn in 1893. He repeated this subject, with some changes in composition, in 1894 (Gemeentemuseum, The Hague).

THEODOOR VAN HOYTEMA. B. The Hague, 1863; d. 1917. Acquired a reputation as a lithographer illustrating bird books, the first of which appeared in 1892.

211 *Spoonbills in a Wood*. Lithograph in green. Inscribed "Hoytema." Printed in 1898.

WILLEM BASTIAAN THOLEN. B. Amsterdam, 1860; d. The Hague, 1931.

212 *Vats in a Paper Mill at Vaassen*. Black chalk and water color. Inscribed "Tholen." Drawn between 1901 and 1903. Apart from the vats which occur in another composition, Tholen also drew the press, the stampers, the rags, the drying shed, the storehouse, and the factory's waterpower installation. All the studies, more than 20 altogether, are in the Museum Boymans, Rotterdam.

PIETER DUPONT. B. Amsterdam, 1870; d. Hilversum, 1911. Visited Paris in 1890 and 1894, and lived there from 1896 to 1902. From 1902 to 1911 he taught graphic art at the "Rijksacademie."

213 *Bank of the Seine in Paris*. Black and white chalk. Inscribed "Dupont Seine-oever. Paris 1908." Drawn during one of his holiday trips, which invariably took him to France.

JOHAN THORN PRIKKER. B. The Hague, 1868; d. Cologne, 1932. Worked in Germany from 1904 onward.

214 *Les Xhorres*. Wax crayon in color. Inscribed "Les Xhorres." Drawn in 1901. His Pointillist landscapes were all executed between 1901 and 1904 in the neighborhood of Visé, where he spent his summers in those years.

CORNELUS THEODORUS MARIA (KEES) VAN DONGEN. B. Delfshaven, 1877. Has worked in Paris since 1897, acquired French nationality in 1929.

215 *Zandstraat, Rotterdam*. Black chalk and water color. Inscribed "V.D." and "Van Dongen." Drawn in 1899. The Zandstraat was a well-known street in the seamen's quarter, which no longer exists.

216 *The Meuse at Schiedam*. Blue, red, black, and brown chalk. Inscribed "V.D." There is a note on the back: "Rotterdam/de Maas à Schiedam." Drawn about 1905.

BART ANTHONY VAN DER LECK. B. Utrecht, 1876; d. Blaricum, 1958.

217 *Street Scene*. Colored chalk. Inscribed "B. v. d. L. 1906." The composition, which is also known by the name "Dance round the Barrel Organ," can be met with again in a painting made in 1910 and now in a private collection in Wassenaar.

JOHANNES CAROLUS BERNARDUS (JAN) SLUYTERS. B. 's-Hertogenbosch, 1881; d. Amsterdam, 1957.

218 *Young Woman*. Brush and chalk over pencil. Signed (twice) "Jan Sluyters," at the top, in red chalk. Drawn about 1912. The model is Sluyters's bride, shortly before their marriage.

219 *Couple Dancing*. Black chalk and brush. Inscribed "JS" (ligature). Made in 1906, as he was returning to Holland from Rome by way of Spain and Paris. A painting with related composition and dated "1906" is preserved in the Stedelijk Museum, Amsterdam.

LODEWIJK SCHELFHOUT. B. The Hague, 1881; d. Amsterdam, 1943.

220 *Les Angles*. Brush, Inscribed "Les Angles. 1911. L. Schelfhout." Drawn 1911-12 during his stay in the south of France in the neighborhood of Avignon.

LEENDERT (LEO) GESTEL. B. Woerden, 1881; d. Blaricum, 1941.

221 *Sailboats, Majorca*. Black chalk. Made during his visit to Majorca from January to May 1914. He also made oil paintings of the same theme and of a number of harbor views (Rijksmuseum Kröller-Müller). This is a page from a sketchbook kept in the same museum.

PIETER CORNELIS (PIET) MONDRIAN. B. Amersfoort, 1872; d. New York, 1944. Lived in Paris (1919-38), London, and New York.

222 *Study of a Tree*. An early version of a series of tree studies, three of them drawn and three painted, which were made in 1909 and 1910. A later series, made in 1911 and 1912, uses the same tree as model. Executed in Domburg.

223 *Study of a Nude*. Charcoal. Drawn in 1912 during the first year of his first stay in Paris (December 1911–summer 1914).

224 *Façade of the Church at Domburg*. Charcoal. Drawn in 1914 after his return from his first stay in Paris. The painter, who spent his summers from 1908 to 1911 in Domburg, repeatedly painted and drew this same motif. The series as a whole demonstrates beautifully his transition from naturalism to pure (abstract) art.

SHORT BIBLIOGRAPHY

Much information on drawings and prints can be found in periodicals and in the material published by print rooms and private collectors about their own collections. A further source is provided by the catalogues of auctions and exhibitions.

Here follows an extremely condensed list of other publications:

REFERENCE BOOKS

H. van Hall, Repertorium voor de geschiedenis der Nederlandsche schilder- en graveerkunst sedert het begin der 12e eeuw tot het eind van 1946, 2 vols. The Hague, 1936 (I), 1949 (II).

F. G. Waller, Biografisch woordenboek van Noord-nederlandse graveurs. The Hague, 1938.

DRAWINGS

GENERAL:
M. D. Henkel, Le dessin hollandais des origines au XVIIe siècle. Paris, 1931.
SPECIAL:
A. E. Popham, Drawings of the Early Flemish School. London, 1926.
J. H. J. Mellaart, Dutch Drawings of the Seventeenth Century. London, 1926.
J.Q. van Regteren Altena, Holländische Meisterzeichnungen. Basel, 1946.
W. Bernt, Die niederländischen Zeichner des 17. Jahrhunderts (A. Koninck). Munich, 1957. Volume II in preparation.
O. Benesch, The Drawings of Rembrandt. 6 vols. London, 1954-57.
J. B. de la Faille, L'œuvre de Vincent van Gogh (Vols III and IV, Drawings). Paris, 1928.
M. Seuphor, Life and Work of Mondrian. New York, 1956.

PRINTS

GENERAL:
A. M. Hind, A History of Engraving and Etching from the 15th Century to the Year 1914. London, 1923 (2nd edition).
F. W. H. Hollstein, Dutch and Flemish Etchings, Engravings and Woodcuts. Amsterdam, 1949-56 (A - Mon, I-XIII, following volumes in preparation).
SPECIAL:
M. J. Schretlen, Flemish and Dutch Woodcuts of the Fifteenth Century. London, 1925.
A. J. J. Delen, Histoire de la gravure dans les anciens Pays-Bas et dans les provinces belges. Paris and Brussels, 1924-35 (3 vols., only 15th and 16th centuries).
L. Münz, A Critical Catalogue of Rembrandt's Etchings, 2 vols. London, 1952.
G. Sluyter, De moderne grafiek in Nederland en Vlaanderen. Amsterdam, 1928.

TECHNIQUE

For drawing techniques the reader is referred to:
A. E. Popham, A Handbook to the Drawings and Water Colours in the Department of Prints and Drawings, British Museum. London, 1939.
J. Meder, Die Handzeichnung, ihre Technik und Entwicklung. Vienna, 1923 (2nd edition).
For engraving techniques see:
A. M. Hind, A Guide to the Processes and Schools of Engraving. London, 1933 (3rd edition).

COLLECTORS OF PRINTS AND DRAWINGS

All data concerning collections and collectors of prints and drawings have now been brought together in:
Frits Lugt, Les marques de collections de dessins et d'estampes. Amsterdam, 1921. Reprinted with Supplement, The Hague, 1957.

SOURCES OF PHOTOGRAPHS

The prints and drawings illustrated in this book have been reproduced with the willing coöperation of public museums and private collectors both in Holland and abroad.

A. Frequin, The Hague, made the photographs kindly furnished by the Museum Boymans: 1, 25, 105, 106, 144, 152, 175, 185, 212, 215, 216, and also: 154, 158, 165, 174, 180.

The Department of Fine Arts of the Municipality of The Hague supplied the following photographs of prints and drawings in the Gemeentemuseum, The Hague: 203, 211, 220. It also supplied the photographs 176 and 177.

The Municipal Museums, Amsterdam, supplied the following photographs: VI, 85, 122, 135, 140, 145, 148, 151, 182, 184, 188, 189, 192, 193, 194, 196, 197, 199, 200, 201, 208.

F. Lugt, Paris, made the following photographs from his own collection: 7, 32, 37, 83, 89, 95, 97. He also made: 26, 107, 113, 146.

The Photographic Committee of the Rijksmuseum, Amsterdam, made available the following photographs of prints and drawings from the Rijksprentenkabinet: II, III, IV, V, 8, 17, 18, 19, 20, 27, 29, 36, 38, 42, 43, 44, 45, 46, 47, 48, 49, 50, 51, 52, 75, 76, 77, 78, 79, 80, 81, 82, 92, 93, 110, 111, 112, 114, 120, 125, 126, 137, 142, 149, 153, 168, 170, 209, 213, and also: 69, 147, 157.

Studio Nico Zomer, Haarlem, made the following photographs in Teyler's Museum, Haarlem: 21, 54, 64, 100, 102, 143, and also: 150.

Reproductions were made from photographs supplied by the following:
A. C. L., Brussels: 28. Archives Photographiques, Paris: 65, 84. Photographie Bernard, Chantilly: 88, 91, 103, 119, 131. Piet Boonstra, Groningen: 141. J. E. Bulloz, Paris: 90. G. Busch-Hauck, Frankfort: 35, 118. Adr. Bijl, Amsterdam: 156, 202. Cooper, London: 104. A. Dingjan, The Hague: 127, 130, 163, 166, 172, 173, 191. John R. Freeman & Co., London: 22. Hessische Treuhandverwaltung, Wiesbaden: 4, 13, 15, 124, 128, 132. Kleinhempel Fotowerkstatten, Hamburg: 16, 56. Foto-Kino Kraaijenzang, Goor: 129. Lichtbeeldeninstituut, Amsterdam: 23, 74, 94, 115, 205. Erich Mauersberger, Marburg: 136. Fototechnische Dienst N.V. Philips Gloeilanpenfabrieken: 167. M. Rigal, Paris: 101. Walter Steinkopf, Berlin-Dahlem: 72, 108. Fotobureau Chr. Stijns, Dordrecht: 155, 162.

PLATES

1. The Master of Zwolle, The Madonna and Child with Cherries. Engraving; $8\frac{7}{8}'' \times 6''$.* Museum Boymans, Rotterdam

2. Hieronymus Bosch, Tree-man. Pen-and-ink drawing; $10\frac{7}{8}'' \times 8\frac{7}{16}''$. * Albertina, Vienna

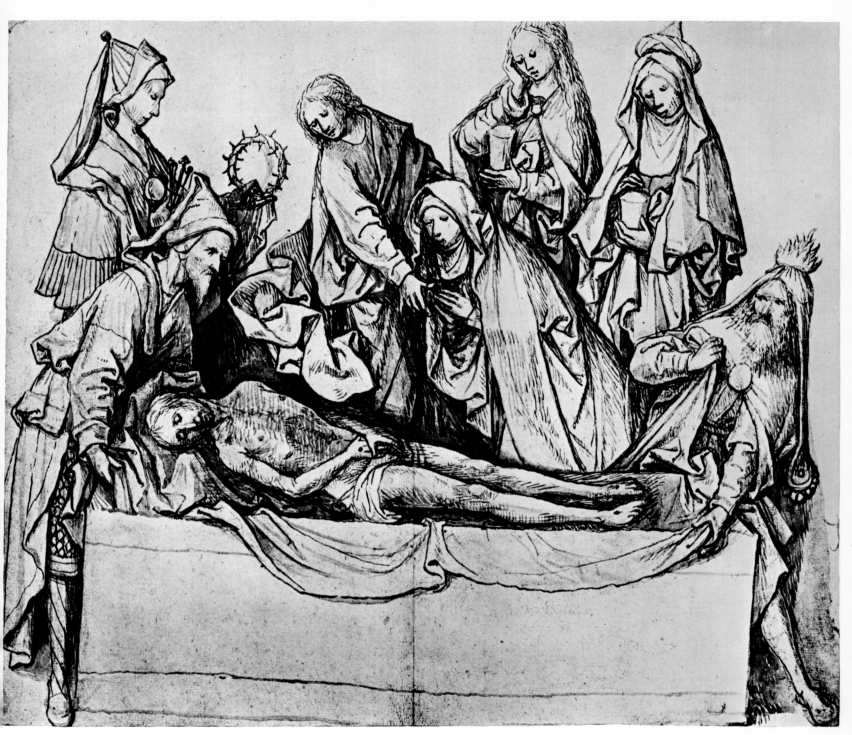

3. Hieronymus Bosch, The Entombment. Brush drawing; $9\frac{13}{16}'' \times 13\frac{3}{4}''$. British Museum, London

4. Hieronymus Bosch, Monsters. Pen-and-ink drawing; $3\frac{3}{8}'' \times 7\frac{5}{16}''$.*Kupferstichkabinett, Berlin

5. Allaert du Hameel, The Raising of the Brazen Serpent. Engraving; $10\frac{3}{8}'' \times 7\frac{3}{8}''$.* Albertina, Vienna

6. Jacob Cornelisz van Amsterdam, Scenes from the Life of the Virgin. 1507; woodcut; $14\frac{1}{16}'' \times 9\frac{7}{16}''$. Bibliothèque Nationale, Paris

7. Lucas van Leyden, The Raising of Lazarus. Engraving; $11\frac{1}{4}'' \times 8''$. *Frits Lugt Collection, Paris

8. Lucas van Leyden, Ecce Homo. 1510; engraving; $11\frac{3}{8}'' \times 17\frac{15}{16}''$. Rijksprentenkabinet, Amsterdam

9. Lucas van Leyden, The Joys of this World and Mary Magdalene. 1519; engraving; $11\frac{1}{2}'' \times 15\frac{9}{16}''$. British Museum, London

10. Lucas van Leyden, A Girl Reading. Chalk drawing; $11\frac{15}{16}'' \times 7\frac{1}{4}''$. * Albertina, Vienna

11. Lucas van Leyden, Portrait of a Young Man. 1521; chalk drawing; $10\frac{1}{4}'' \times 13\frac{3}{4}''$. Lakenhal, Leiden

12. Lucas van Leyden, Man Drawing. Chalk drawing; $10\frac{11}{16}'' \times 10\frac{11}{16}''$. British Museum, London

13. Maerten van Heemskerck, Obelisk of St. Peter's near St. Peter's and Santa Maria delle Febre. Pen-and-ink drawing; $5\frac{1}{16}'' \times 7\frac{7}{8}''$. Kupferstichkabinett, Berlin

14. Jan van Scorel, The Bridge. Pen-and-ink drawing; $8\frac{1}{8}'' \times 6\frac{1}{16}''$. British Museum, London

15. Maerten van Heemskerck, Palatine with Colosseum in the Background. Pen-and-ink drawing; $11\frac{1}{16}'' \times 9\frac{5}{16}''$.
Kupferstichkabinett, Berlin

16. Pieter Aertsz, The Adoration of the Shepherds (design for a window). 1563; pen-and-ink drawing; $15\frac{3}{4}'' \times 7\frac{1}{2}''$.
Kunsthalle, Hamburg

17. Dirck Crabeth, Head of a Man. Chalk drawing; 11$\frac{5}{16}$″ × 8$\frac{11}{16}$″. * Rijksprentenkabinet, Amsterdam

18. Dirck Barendsz, Venetian Ball. 1574; pen-and-wash drawing; $15\frac{3}{4}'' \times 29\frac{1}{8}''$. Rijksprentenkabinet, Amsterdam

19. Cornelis Ketel, Corporation Piece (preparatory sketch). Pen-and-wash drawing; $11\frac{7}{16}'' \times 15\frac{3}{8}''$. Rijksprentenkabinet, Amsterdam

Illus: Generoso et Magnifico Domino Dño
Paulo sexto Trautson libero Baroni in
Sprechenstain et Schrofenstain &c. Sacre,
Cæs: M.tis Camerario, supremo Curiæ Mareschalco,
et Concily Imperialis Præsidi, Dño suo B. Spranger fuit, et H. Goltzius sculp, hæc kneupli animi,
humilisq; obsequy Mnemosynon quantuluciq; D.D.

O homo qui cernis nostrum sub imagine funus,   Authorem venerata suum, et testata dolorem   Obtexit rutulos et Sol caligine vultus,   (ten
Esto memor quam sim pro te crudelia passus,   Intremuit tellus magno concussa fragore,   Et stupuit Natura parens miserata Paren
Qui fueram plastes, fierem saluator vt idem.   Et tum nec silices, nec saxa carentia sensu.   Nec gemitum vos ô cæli tenuistis Alumni.

Franco Estius copos.

20. Hendrick Goltzius, Christ Borne from the Tomb by Angels (after B. Spranger). 1587; copper engraving; 13¾″ × 9¹⁵⁄₁₆″.
Rijksprentenkabinet, Amsterdam

21. Hendrick Goltzius, Portrait of Giovanni da Bologna. 1591; chalk drawing; $14\frac{9}{16}''\times11\frac{13}{16}''$. Teyler's Museum, Haarlem

22. Hendrick Goltzius, Study of a Tree. Pen-and-wash drawing; $16\frac{15}{16}'' \times 11\frac{13}{16}''$. F. F. Madan Collection, London

23. Roeland Saverij, Study of a Tree. Chalk drawing; 19″×14⅝″. Collection Professor J. Q. van Regteren Altena, Amsterdam

24. Jacob de Gheyn II, Landscape with Highway Robbery. 1603; pen-and-ink drawing; $9\frac{3}{8}'' \times 15\frac{3}{8}''$. Staatliche Graphische Sammlung, Munich

25. Hendrick Goltzius, Landscape with Dunes near Haarlem. 1603; pen-and-ink drawing; $3\frac{1}{2}'' \times 6''$.* Museum Boymans, Rotterdam

26. Abraham Bloemaert, Studies of Garden Plants. Pen-and-ink drawing; $11\frac{3}{8}'' \times 14\frac{7}{8}''$. Ecole des Beaux-Arts, Paris

27. Jacob de Gheyn II, Studies of a Field Mouse. Pen-and-brush drawing; $5\frac{1}{16}'' \times 7\frac{3}{16}''$. Rijksprentenkabinet, Amsterdam

28. Jacob de Gheyn II, Nude Studies. Pen-and-chalk drawing; 10⅜″ × 13″. Musées Royaux des Beaux-Arts, Brussels

29. Jacob de Gheyn II, Woman with Death. 1600; pen-and-ink drawing; 6⁵⁄₁₆″ × 5⅛″. Rijksprentenkabinet, Amsterdam

30. Jacob de Gheyn II, Portrait. Leadpoint-and-red-chalk drawing; 6″ × 5¼″. Coll. Prof. J. Q. van Regteren Altena, Amsterdam

31. Balthasar van der Ast, Still Life with Fruit and Shells. Colored pen-and-ink drawing; $10\frac{13}{16}'' \times 15\frac{3}{16}''$. British Museum, London

32. Jacob de Gheyn II, Studies of Insects. 1600; colored pen-and-ink drawing; $8\frac{7}{8}'' \times 6\frac{7}{8}''$. Frits Lugt Collection, Paris

33. Jan van de Velde, Fish Market. Pen-and-ink drawing; $12\frac{11}{16}'' \times 22\frac{1}{16}''$. Albertina, Vienna

34. Claes Jansz Visscher, Loenersloot. Pen-and-ink drawing; $7\frac{11}{16}'' \times 12\frac{1}{8}''$. Statens Museum for Kunst, Copenhagen

35. Hendrick Averkamp, Winter Landscape. Colored pen-and-ink drawing; $6\frac{5}{8}'' \times 12\frac{3}{8}''$. Städelsches Kunstinstitut, Frankfort

36. Hendrick Averkamp, Duck Hunter (sketch). Pencil drawing; $6\frac{13}{16}'' \times 4\frac{5}{8}''$.* Rijksprentenkabinet, Amsterdam

37. Jan Anthonisz van Ravesteyn, Civic Guard of the Company of St. Sebastian, The Hague (preparatory sketch).
    1618; pen-and-wash drawing; $9\frac{3}{4}'' \times 20\frac{3}{8}''$. Frits Lugt Collection, Paris

38. Gerard Terborgh the Elder, The Tiber with the Ponte Rotto, Rome. 1609; pen-and-ink drawing; $6\frac{3}{16}'' \times 9\frac{3}{4}''$.
    Rijksprentenkabinet, Amsterdam

39. Thomas de Keyser, Civic Guard (preparatory sketch). Pen-and-wash drawing; $7\frac{7}{8}'' \times 16\frac{1}{16}''$. Statens Museum for Kunst, Copenhagen

40. Gerard van Honthorst, The Four Elements. Pen-and-wash drawing; $7\frac{7}{8}'' \times 10\frac{7}{8}''$. Centraal Museum, Utrecht

41. Willem Buytewegh, Standing Cavalier. Chalk drawing; 15¾″ × 9⁷⁄₁₆″. Museum Boymans, Rotterdam

42. Frans Hals (attributed to), Cavalier. Chalk drawing; 16⅟₁₆″×9″. Rijksprentenkabinet, Amsterdam

43. Willem Jacobsz Delff, Cavalcade of the Princes of Nassau (after Adriaen van der Venne). 1621; engraving; $17\frac{1}{8}'' \times 22\frac{7}{16}''$. Rijksprentenkabinet, Amsterdam

Mavors quiescit laureatus altius
Quiescat in Bonum usquè et usquè publicum.

44. Willem Buytewegh, Gunner and Camp Follower. Etching; $5\frac{9}{16}'' \times 3\frac{11}{16}''$. Rijksprentenkabinet, Amsterdam

45. Jacob de Gheyn III, Sleeping Mars. Etching; $7\frac{1}{2}'' \times 6\frac{1}{4}''$. Rijksprentenkabinet, Amsterdam

ESAIAS VANDEN VELDE Fecit.
I.P. Beerendrecht. excudit. Haerlemensu

46. Esaias van de Velde, Woods with Country Road. Etching; $6\frac{3}{4}'' \times 6\frac{7}{8}''$.*Rijksprentenkabinet, Amsterdam

47. Willem Buytewegh, Trees by the Water. 1616; etching; $3\frac{1}{2}'' \times 4\frac{7}{8}''$.*Rijksprentenkabinet, Amsterdam

48. Hercules Seghers, Two Trees with Fresh Foliage. Etching; 6″×6¾″.*Rijksprentenkabinet, Amsterdam

49. Hercules Seghers, Mossy Larch Tree. Etching; 6⅝″×3⅞″. Rijksprentenkabinet, Amsterdam

50. Hercules Seghers, Rocky Landscape with River. Etching; $5\frac{9}{16}'' \times 7\frac{7}{8}''$. Rijksprentenkabinet, Amsterdam

51. Hercules Seghers, Still Life with Three Books. Etching; $3\frac{5}{8}'' \times 7\frac{7}{8}''$.* Rijksprentenkabinet, Amsterdam

52. Hercules Seghers, The Great Tree. Etching; $8\frac{5}{8}'' \times 11''$. *Rijksprentenkabinet, Amsterdam

53. Hercules Seghers, Rocky Landscape with Four Trees. Etching; $11\frac{5}{16}'' \times 18\frac{9}{16}''$. British Museum, London

54. Gerard Terborgh the Younger, Haarlem Town Hall and Market. Chalk and pen-and-wash drawing; $7\frac{5}{16}'' \times 10\frac{13}{16}''$.
Teyler's Museum, Haarlem

55. Pieter Saenredam, Haarlem Market Place. 1629; pen-and-ink drawing; $5'' \times 7\frac{5}{8}''$.*Koninklijke Bibliotheek, The Hague

56. Cornelis Vroom, Forest Road. Colored pen-and-ink drawing; $13\frac{11}{16}'' \times 11\frac{11}{16}''$. Kunsthalle, Hamburg

57. Rembrandt, Portrait of the Artist's Father. Chalk-and-wash drawing; $7\frac{7}{16}'' \times 9\frac{7}{16}''$. Ashmolean Museum, Oxford

58. Rembrandt, Self Portrait. Pen-and-brush drawing;
$5'' \times 3\frac{3}{4}''$. British Museum, London

59. Rembrandt, Portrait of the Artist's Mother. Pen-and-brush
drawing; $4\frac{3}{4}'' \times 4\frac{1}{4}''$. A. Strölin Collection, Lausanne

60. Rembrandt, Saskia with Child. Pen-and-wash drawing; $7\frac{3}{8}'' \times 5\frac{3}{8}''$. Pierpont Morgan Library, New York

61. Rembrandt, Hendrickje Stoffels. 1645; chalk drawing; $3\frac{5}{16}'' \times 2\frac{5}{8}''$.* Count Antoine Seilern Collection, London

62. Rembrandt, Christ Carrying the Cross. Pen-and-brush drawing; $5\frac{11}{16}'' \times 10\frac{1}{4}''$. Kupferstichkabinett, Berlin

63. Rembrandt, The Crucifixion. Pen-and-ink drawing; $6\frac{1}{2}'' \times 9\frac{3}{8}''$. Städelsches Kunstinstitut, Frankfort

64. Rembrandt, The Return of the Prodigal Son. Pen-and-wash drawing; $7\frac{1}{2}'' \times 8\frac{15}{16}''$. Teyler's Museum, Haarlem

65. Rembrandt, View of the Singel at Amersfoort. Pen-and-wash drawing; 6″ × 10⅞″.*Louvre, Paris

66. Rembrandt, Two Farmhouses. Pen-and-wash drawing; $7\frac{1}{2}'' \times 12''$.*Kupferstichkabinett, Berlin

67. Rembrandt, Lioness Devouring a Bird. Chalk-and-wash drawing; 5″×9⁷⁄₁₆″. British Museum, London

68. Rembrandt, Oriental Horseman (after an Indian miniature). Colored pen-and-chalk drawing; 10⁷⁄₈″×8¹⁄₈″. British Museum, London

69. Rembrandt, Homer Reciting Poetry. 1652; pen-and-ink drawing; $10\frac{1}{16}'' \times 7\frac{3}{16}''$.* Six Foundation, Amsterdam

70. Rembrandt, Female Nude from the Back. Pen-and-wash drawing; $9\frac{1}{8}" \times 7\frac{3}{16}"$. *The Art Institute of Chicago

71. Rembrandt, Sleeping Young Woman (Hendrickje). Brush drawing; $9\frac{11}{16}'' \times 8\frac{1}{16}''$. *British Museum, London

72. Rembrandt, Christ Raising Jairus's Daughter. Pen-and-ink drawing; $7\frac{15}{16}'' \times 7\frac{3}{4}''$. *Formerly W. Bode Collection, Berlin

73. Rembrandt, Christ and the Woman Taken in Adultery. Pen-and-ink drawing; $3\frac{15}{16}'' \times 6\frac{9}{16}''$. Wallraf-Richartz Museum, Cologne

74. Rembrandt, Portrait of "Jan Six." Reed pen; $9\frac{1}{8}'' \times 7\frac{11}{16}''$.*Six Foundation, Amsterdam

75. Rembrandt, Annunciation to the Shepherds. 1634; etching; $10\frac{5}{16}''\times8\frac{5}{8}''$.* Rijksprentenkabinet, Amsterdam

76. Rembrandt, The "Six" Bridge. 1645; etching; $4\frac{15}{16}'' \times 8\frac{3}{4}''$.* Rijksprentenkabinet, Amsterdam

77. Rembrandt, The Hunter. 1653; etching; $5\frac{1}{16}'' \times 6\frac{3}{16}''$.* Rijksprentenkabinet, Amsterdam

78. Rembrandt, "Hundred Guilder Print." Etching; $11\frac{1}{16}'' \times 15\frac{9}{16}''$. Rijksprentenkabinet, Amsterdam

79. Rembrandt, The Three Crosses. 1653; etching (fourth state); 15¼″ × 17¾″. Rijksprentenkabinet, Amsterdam

80. Rembrandt, Reclining Nude. 1658; etching; $3\frac{1}{8}'' \times 6\frac{3}{16}''$. * Rijksprentenkabinet, Amsterdam

81. Rembrandt, Seated Nude. 1658; etching; $6\frac{3}{16}'' \times 4\frac{15}{16}''$. * Rijksprentenkabinet, Amsterdam

82. Rembrandt, Portrait of Dr. Arnold Tholinx. 1656; etching; $7\frac{7}{8}'' \times 5\frac{15}{16}''$.* Rijksprentenkabinet, Amsterdam

83. Ferdinand Bol, Hagar in the Wilderness. Pen-and-ink drawing; $11\frac{7}{16}'' \times 7\frac{1}{16}''$. *Frits Lugt Collection, Paris

84. Barend Fabritius, Judas Returning the Pieces of Silver. Pen-and-brush drawing; $6\frac{5}{16}''\times9\frac{7}{16}''$. Louvre, Paris

85. Gerard Dou, An Old Man Cutting His Quill. Chalk drawing; $9\frac{3}{8}''\times7\frac{3}{16}''$. Museum Fodor, Amsterdam

86. Govert Flinck, Studies of a Peacock. Chalk-and-brush drawing; 11¾″×8¾″.*Collection Goldsche 1935, Berlin

87. Jacob Backer, Reclining Nude. Chalk drawing; $7\frac{5}{16}'' \times 13\frac{11}{16}''$. Prentenkabinet, University of Leiden

88. Nicolaes Maes, Girl with Basket. Chalk drawing; $8\frac{1}{16}'' \times 5\frac{1}{2}''$. Musée Condé, Chantilly

89. Jan Lievens, Portrait of Gaspard Streso. Chalk drawing; $9\frac{1}{8}'' \times 7\frac{11}{16}''$. *Frits Lugt Collection, Paris

90. Gerbrandt van den Eeckhout, Boy Sitting on a Chair. Brush drawing; $10\frac{1}{4}'' \times 7\frac{3}{16}''$. * Cognacq Jay Museum, Paris

91. Lambert Doomer, The Castle at Saumur. Pen-and-wash drawing; $9\frac{1}{8}'' \times 16\frac{3}{16}''$. Musée Condé, Chantilly

92. Anthonie van Borssum, Windmill and Rolling Bridge. Colored pen-and-ink drawing; $8'' \times 13\frac{3}{16}''$. Rijksprentenkabinet, Amsterdam

93. Jan Lievens, Forest Scene with Stag. Pen-and-ink drawing; $9\frac{5}{16}'' \times 15\frac{1}{4}''$. Rijksprentenkabinet, Amsterdam

94. Abraham Furnerius, Forest Scene with Road. Chalk and pen-and-wash drawing; $7\frac{1}{16}'' \times 11\frac{5}{8}''$. Collection C. P. van Eeghen, Amsterdam

95. Adriaen van Ostade, Study for a Family Group Portrait. Pen-and-wash drawing; $6\frac{1}{4}'' \times 8''$.* Frits Lugt Collection, Paris

96. Adriaen van Ostade, Backgammon Players. Pen-and-wash drawing; $5\frac{1}{2}'' \times 7\frac{9}{16}''$. British Museum, London

97. Isaac van Ostade, Adoration of the Shepherds. Pen-and-wash drawing; $6\frac{1}{4}'' \times 8\frac{1}{2}''$. *Frits Lugt Collection, Paris

98. Jan Steen, Gay Company in an Arbor. Chalk and pen-and-wash drawing; $7\frac{15}{16}'' \times 9\frac{13}{16}''$. Albertina, Vienna

99. Jan van Goyen, Landscape with a Windmill. 1644; chalk drawing; $5\frac{7}{8}'' \times 10\frac{1}{4}''$. Courtauld Institute, London

100. Albert Cuyp, Landscape with River and Cows. Chalk drawing; $8\frac{1}{4}'' \times 17\frac{15}{16}''$. Teyler's Museum, Haarlem

101. Aert van der Neer, Landscape with Three Farmhouses. Brush drawing; $7\frac{1}{2}'' \times 12\frac{3}{8}''$. Louvre, Paris

102. Jan van de Cappelle, Golf-playing on the Ice. Brush drawing; $6'' \times 8\frac{1}{4}''$.* Teyler's Museum, Haarlem

103. Philips Koninck, Distant View with River. Pen-and-wash drawing; $7\frac{5}{8}'' \times 12\frac{3}{8}''$. Frits Lugt Collection, Paris

104. Albert Cuyp, Wooded Landscape. Chalk-and-wash drawing; $7\frac{5}{8}'' \times 12\frac{3}{16}''$. Pierpont Morgan Library, New York

105. Jacob van Ruisdael, Forest Scene. Etching; $7\frac{3}{16}'' \times 10\frac{5}{8}''$. Museum Boymans, Rotterdam

106. Jacob van Ruisdael, Grainfield. Etching; $4\frac{1}{16}'' \times 6''$.*Museum Boymans, Rotterdam

107. Jacob van Ruisdael, Interior of the Old Church, Amsterdam. Chalk-and-wash drawing; $19'' \times 16\frac{5}{16}''$. Ecole des Beaux-Arts, Paris

108. Jacob van Ruisdael, View of a Beach. Chalk-and-wash drawing; $9\frac{1}{16}'' \times 14\frac{7}{8}''$. Kupferstichkabinett, Berlin

109. Allaert van Everdingen, Mountain Landscape in Sweden. Pen-and-wash drawing; $13\frac{3}{4}'' \times 16\frac{1}{8}''$. The Fogg Museum of Art, Cambridge, Mass.

110. Reinier Nooms, The Element of Air. Etching; $3\frac{5}{16}'' \times 7\frac{7}{8}''$.*Rijksprentenkabinet, Amsterdam

111. Reinier Nooms, The Element of Water. Etching; $3\frac{1}{16}'' \times 7\frac{7}{8}''$.*Rijksprentenkabinet, Amsterdam

112. Allaert van Everdingen, Coastal Landscape with Rocks. Etching; $3\frac{15}{16}'' \times 5\frac{7}{8}''$.*Rijksprentenkabinet, Amsterdam

113. Meindert Hobbema, Church and Watermill at Deventer. Chalk-and-wash drawing; $6\frac{3}{4}'' \times 11\frac{5}{8}''$.* Petit Palais, Paris

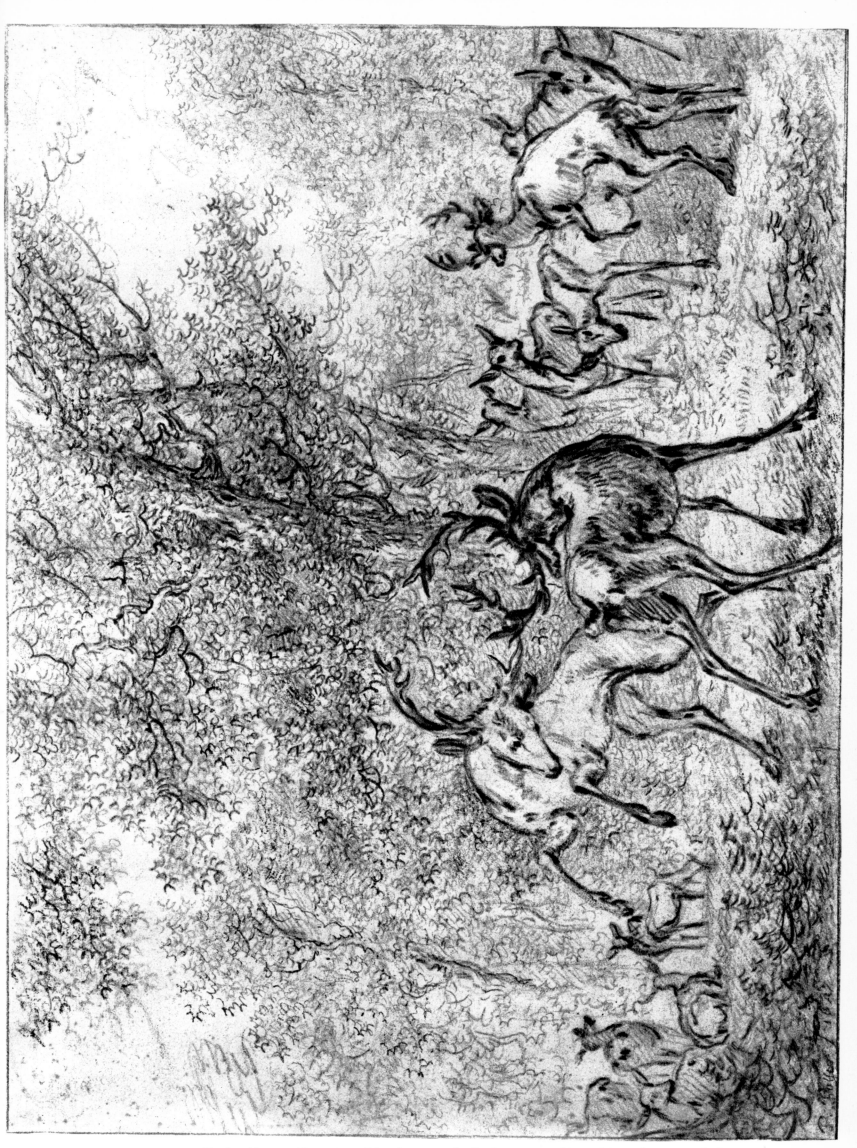

114. Paulus Potter, Deer in a Wood. 1647; chalk drawing; 9⅜″ × 12 9/16″. Rijksprentenkabinet, Amsterdam

115. Bartholomeus van der Helst, Man Seated. Chalk drawing; $7\frac{11}{16}'' \times 5\frac{9}{16}''$.* Collection Professor J. Q. van Regteren Altena, Amsterdam

116. Anthonie Waterloo, Oude Gracht in Utrecht. Chalk-and-wash drawing; $11\frac{13}{16}'' \times 16\frac{1}{8}''$. Victoria and Albert Museum, London

117. Roeland Roghman, The Castle at Wijk bij Duurstede. Chalk-and-wash drawing; $7\frac{1}{16}'' \times 10\frac{5}{8}''$. Albertina, Vienna

118. Gabriël Metsu, Woman with a Silver Basin. Chalk drawing; 9$\frac{13}{16}$″ × 5$\frac{3}{4}$″.* Städelsches Kunstinstitut, Frankfort

119. Adriaen van de Velde, Two Country Girls. Chalk drawing; $11\frac{15}{16}'' \times 7\frac{1}{4}''$. *Frits Lugt Collection, Paris

120. Jan de Bray, Portrait of a Girl. 1663; chalk drawing; $4\frac{11}{16}'' \times 3\frac{3}{4}''$. Rijksprentenkabinet, Amsterdam

121. Cornelis Visscher, Head of a Boy. Chalk drawing; $5\frac{3}{8}'' \times 4\frac{7}{6}''$. The Fogg Museum of Art, Cambridge, Mass.

122. Caspar Netscher, Girl with a Top. Chalk drawing; $4\frac{7}{16}'' \times 4\frac{3}{4}''$.* Museum Fodor, Amsterdam

123. Caspar Netscher, Young Woman at a Window. Pen-and-wash drawing; $9\frac{1}{8}" \times 7"$. *Pierpont Morgan Library, New York

124. Bartholomeus Breenbergh, View of Tivoli. 1625; pen-and-wash drawing; $11\frac{3}{8}'' \times 10\frac{11}{16}''$. Kupferstichkabinett, Berlin

125. Jan Both, View in the Campagna Showing the Tiber. Etching; $7\frac{5}{8}'' \times 10\frac{11}{16}''$. Rijksprentenkabinet, Amsterdam

126. Nicolaes Berchem, Man Riding a Mule. 1644; etching; $6\frac{5}{8}'' \times 7\frac{5}{16}''$. Rijksprentenkabinet, Amsterdam

127. Jan de Bisschop, Two Persons Sketching at Zorgvliet, The Hague. Pen-and-wash drawing; $9\frac{5}{8}'' \times 14\frac{11}{16}''$. Gemeentearchief, The Hague

128. Valentijn Klotz, View of Maastricht. 1671; pen-and-wash drawing; $10\frac{5}{8}'' \times 12\frac{5}{8}''$. Kupferstichkabinett, Berlin

129. Jan van der Heyden, Firemen at a Fire. Pen-and-wash drawing; $12\frac{5}{8}'' \times 17\frac{3}{4}''$. Collection A. C. van Eck, Delden

130. Constantijn Huygens, View of The Hague. 1666; pen-and-brush drawing; $8\frac{9}{16}'' \times 15\frac{3}{16}''$.
Estate of Jonkheer Dr. W. A. Beelaerts van Blokland

131. Willem van de Velde the Younger, The IJ at Amsterdam. Pen-and-wash drawing; $6\frac{9}{16}'' \times 10\frac{1}{2}''$. Frits Lugt Collection, Paris

132. Willem van de Velde the Younger, Ship. Pen-and-wash drawing; $9\frac{1}{2}'' \times 7\frac{13}{16}''$. Kupferstichkabinett, Berlin

133. Ludolf Backhuyzen, The Man-of-War *King William* off Rotterdam. 1689; pen-and-wash drawing; $5\frac{1}{2}'' \times 10\frac{1}{16}''$. Albertina, Vienna

134. Ludolf Backhuyzen, Returning Seafarers. Pen-and-wash drawing; $5\frac{3}{4}'' \times 8\frac{7}{16}''$. *Pierpont Morgan Library, New York

135. Cornelis Saftleven, Raccoons. Colored chalk-and-brush drawing; $7\frac{7}{8}'' \times 12\frac{3}{16}''$. Museum Fodor, Amsterdam

136. Albert van den Eeckhout, Brazilian Owl. Chalk-and-brush drawing; $7\frac{5}{16}'' \times 6\frac{11}{16}''$. Formerly Staatsbibliothek, Berlin

137. Herman Saftleven, Cactus. 1683; colored pen-and-ink drawing; 14″ × 10$\frac{1}{16}$″. Rijksprentenkabinet, Amsterdam

138. Maria Sybille Merian, Study of Plant and Insects. Colored brush drawing; $10\frac{1}{16}'' \times 14''$. Prentenkabinet, University of Leiden

139. Aert Schouman, Two Crested Peacocks. 1754; water color; $10\frac{3}{8}'' \times 14\frac{7}{8}''$.
Collection Mr. and Mrs. Fransen van de Putte-Strootman, The Hague

140. Jan Luyken, Herod Making War on the Robbers. Pen-and-brush drawing; $12\frac{5}{8}'' \times 16\frac{9}{16}''$. Museum Fodor, Amsterdam

141. Johannes Glauber, Mountain Landscape. Pen-and-ink drawing; $11\frac{1}{2}'' \times 14\frac{7}{8}''$.
Groninger Museum voor Stad en Ommelanden, Groningen

142. Jacob de Wit, Design for a Ceiling. 1746; pen-and-wash drawing; $19\frac{3}{16}'' \times 13\frac{1}{4}''$. Rijksprentenkabinet, Amsterdam

143. Cornelis Troost, A Reception. Pen-and-wash drawing; $16\frac{1}{8}'' \times 24\frac{3}{16}''$. Teyler's Museum, Haarlem

144. Hendrik Pothoven, Child in High Chair. Chalk drawing; $9\frac{7}{16}'' \times 7\frac{1}{2}''$. Collection Dr. D. Hannema, Goor

145. Cornelis Troost, Portrait of a Girl. Pastel; 14$\frac{15}{16}$″ × 11″. Museum Fodor, Amsterdam

146. Jan van Huysum, Study of Plants and Flowers. 1731; chalk-and-brush drawing; $18\frac{11}{16}'' \times 14''$. Louvre, Paris

147. Jacob Cats, View from the Tafelberg. Colored pen-and-ink drawing; $16\frac{3}{4}'' \times 22\frac{5}{16}''$. Collection C. P. van Eeghen, Amsterdam

148. Reinier Vinkeles, Winter Scene on the Buiten-Amstel near the Beerebijt. 1769; chalk-and-brush drawing; $7\frac{5}{16}'' \times 10\frac{1}{2}''$. Historisch Topografische Atlas, Gemeentearchief, Amsterdam

149. Dirk Langendijk, The Fire in the St. John's Church, Arnhem. Pen-and-wash drawing; $9\frac{1}{2}'' \times 13\frac{3}{8}''$. Rijksprentenkabinet, Amsterdam

150. Wijbrand Hendriks, Maples under the Snow in the Haarlem Woods. Chalk and water color; $15\frac{9}{16}'' \times 16\frac{9}{16}''$. Historisch Topografische Atlas, Gemeentearchief, Haarlem.

151. Simon Fokke, The Utrecht Towboat. Pen-and-brush drawing; $6\frac{1}{4}'' \times 10''$. Historisch Topografische Atlas, Gemeentearchief, Amsterdam

152. Jacobus Perkois, Three Figures. Water color; $11\frac{13}{16}'' \times 9\frac{15}{16}''$. Museum Boymans, Rotterdam

153. Charles Hodges, Two Ladies Making Music. 1806; chalk-and-brush drawing; $15\frac{3}{4}'' \times 12\frac{1}{2}''$. Rijksprentenkabinet, Amsterdam

154. Paulus van Liender, Forest Scene. Pen-and-wash drawing; $14\frac{3}{8}'' \times 18\frac{1}{2}''$. J. Knoef Estate, Amsterdam

155. Jacob van Strij, Summer Scene outside Dordrecht. Brush drawing; $13\frac{1}{8}'' \times 16\frac{9}{16}''$. Dordrechts Museum, Dordrecht

156. Barend Cornelis Koekkoek, Study of Trees. Brush drawing; $12\frac{3}{8}'' \times 8\frac{7}{8}''$. J. Knoef Estate, Amsterdam

157. Jurriaen Andriessen, The Camera Obscura. Pen-and-brush drawing; $10\frac{1}{8}'' \times 7\frac{1}{16}''$.* Rijksprentenkabinet, Amsterdam

158. Wouter van Troostwijk, Man Seated. 1808; pen-and-brush drawing; $9\frac{3}{16}'' \times 7''$.*Frits Lugt Collection, Paris

159. David Humbert de Superville, The Flood. Water color; $26\frac{3}{4}'' \times 40\frac{3}{16}''$. Prentenkabinet, University of Leiden

160. David Humbert de Superville, Ice Floes on the Meuse. 1809; chalk-and-brush drawing; $15\frac{7}{16}'' \times 18\frac{7}{8}''$.
 Prentenkabinet, University of Leiden

161. Simon Krausz, Head of a Calf. Chalk-and-brush drawing; $12\frac{3}{8}'' \times 16\frac{1}{8}''$. Rijksmuseum Kröller-Müller, Otterlo

162. Abraham van Strij, The Connoisseur. Pen-and-wash drawing; $8\frac{7}{16}'' \times 9\frac{13}{16}''$. Gemeentearchief, Dordrecht

163. Wijnand Nuyen, Rue du Gros-Horloge, Rouen. Water color; $16\frac{9}{16}'' \times 11\frac{13}{16}''$. Collection P. A. Scheen, The Hague

164. Johannes Bosboom, Interior of the Geertekerk, Utrecht. Water color; 24″ × 18⅞″. Collection D. van Houten, The Hague

165. Charles Rochussen, Outpost of the Hussars. 1873; water color; $9'' \times 12\frac{7}{8}''$. Royal property, Het Loo

166. Willem Maris, Girl Herding Cows. Water color; $8\frac{11}{16}'' \times 13\frac{3}{8}''$. Collection D. Reuder-Vles, Rotterdam

167. Matthijs Maris, The Royal Children. Charcoal; $19\frac{7}{8}'' \times 13''$. Collection Mr. and Mrs. P. F. S. Otten-Philips, Eindhoven

168. August Allebé, Portrait of Aunt Thérèse. 1858; pencil and water color; $8\frac{9}{16}'' \times 6''$.* Rijksprentenkabinet, Amsterdam

169. Paul Gabriël, Farmyard. Chalk drawing; $18\frac{15}{16}'' \times 12\frac{5}{8}''$. Rijksmuseum Kröller-Müller, Otterlo

170. Jacob Maris, The Schreierstoren, Amsterdam. Charcoal drawing; $8\frac{1}{16}'' \times 13\frac{3}{4}''$. Rijksprentenkabinet, Amsterdam

171. Willem Roelofs, Landscape. Chalk drawing; $6\frac{3}{4}'' \times 13\frac{5}{16}''$. Collection Mrs. A. Roelofs-Blekman, The Hague

172. Anton Mauve, The Sale of Timber. Water color; $13\frac{9}{16}'' \times 20\frac{1}{4}''$. Rijksmuseum H. W. Mesdag, The Hague

173. Johannes Hendrik Weissenbruch, Polder Landscape. Water color; $5\frac{7}{16}'' \times 8\frac{1}{4}''$.*Collection P. A. Scheen, The Hague

174. Johan Barthold Jongkind, The *Jazon* at Rotterdam. 1856; water color; $10\frac{7}{16}'' \times 9\frac{13}{16}''$. Gemeentemuseum, The Hague

175. Johan Barthold Jongkind, The Quays of the Seine in Paris. Water color; $11\frac{15}{16}'' \times 18\frac{9}{16}''$. Museum Boymans, Rotterdam

176. Johan Barthold Jongkind, The Seine near Bas-Meudon. 1866; water color; $8\frac{11}{16}'' \times 18\frac{1}{8}''$. Collection Dr. V. Simon, Paris

177. Johan Barthold Jongkind, View of Grenoble. 1877; water color; $8\frac{7}{8}'' \times 14\frac{3}{16}''$. Rijksmuseum Kröller-Müller, Otterlo

178. Johan Barthold Jongkind, La Côte Saint-André. 1885; water color; $6\frac{5}{8}'' \times 9\frac{1}{16}''$. Rijksmuseum Kröller-Müller, Otterlo

179. George Hendrik Breitner, Galloping Horse Artillery. Water color; $20\frac{1}{16}'' \times 38\frac{3}{16}''$. Collection H. E. ten Cate, Oldenzaal

180. George Hendrik Breitner, Saturday Evening Market in the Rain on the Prinsegracht, The Hague. Water color; $13\frac{3}{4}'' \times 18\frac{1}{2}''$. Collection A. C. van Ommen van Guylik, Laren

181. George Hendrik Breitner, Reclining Nude. Chalk drawing; $4\frac{3}{4}'' \times 12\frac{13}{16}''$. Rijksmuseum Kröller-Müller, Otterlo

182. George Hendrik Breitner, Pile Driving near the IJ, Amsterdam. 1897; chalk-and-brush drawing; $19\frac{5}{16}'' \times 17\frac{1}{8}''$. Rijksmuseum Kröller-Müller, Otterlo

183. Jozef Israëls, Woman Drinking Coffee. Chalk drawing; $7\frac{7}{16}'' \times 12\frac{1}{2}''$. Rijksmuseum Kröller-Müller, Otterlo

184. Suze Bisschop-Robertson, Boy Sitting on a Bench. Chalk drawing; $16\frac{1}{8}'' \times 12\frac{5}{8}''$. Collection Mrs. S. Eckhart-Bisschop, The Hague

185. Marius Bauer, The Horses of San Marco, Venice. 1895; chalk drawing; $11\frac{7}{16}'' \times 13\frac{1}{16}''$. Collection Mrs. J. Bauer-Stumpff, Amsterdam

186. Willem de Zwart, Girl Reading. Chalk drawing; $11\frac{5}{8}'' \times 11''\frac{5}{8}$. Rijksmuseum Kröller-Müller, Otterlo

187. Isaäc Israëls, Lady with Cigarette, Reading. Water color; 20″ × 13⅞″. Rijksmuseum Kröller-Müller, Otterlo

188. Vincent van Gogh, Mother and Child. 1883; charcoal, chalk and pencil-and-wash drawing; $21\frac{1}{16}'' \times 13\frac{3}{4}''$.
Collection V. W. van Gogh, Stedelijk Museum, Amsterdam

189. Vincent van Gogh, The Gravedigger. 1885; chalk drawing; $13\frac{9}{16}'' \times 8\frac{1}{4}''$. Collection V. W. van Gogh, Stedelijk Museum, Amsterdam

190. Vincent van Gogh, Behind the Schenkweg, The Hague. 1882; pen, chalk, and brush drawing; $11\frac{3}{16}'' \times 18\frac{1}{2}''$.
Rijksmuseum Kröller-Müller, Otterlo

191. Vincent van Gogh, Landscape at Nuenen. 1884; pen-and-ink and body color; $15\frac{3}{8}'' \times 20\frac{7}{8}''$.
Collection Mr. and Mrs. H. Polak-Leyden, Wassenaar

192. Vincent van Gogh, The Grote Markt at Antwerp. 1885; chalk drawing; $8\frac{7}{8}'' \times 11\frac{13}{16}''$. Collection V. W. van Gogh, Stedelijk Museum, Amsterdam

193. Vincent van Gogh, Dead Sparrows. 1886; chalk drawing; $9\frac{7}{16}'' \times 12\frac{5}{8}''$. Collection V. W. van Gogh, Stedelijk Museum, Amsterdam

194. Vincent van Gogh, Summerhouse with Sunflower. Paris, 1887; pen and water color; $12\frac{3}{8}'' \times 9\frac{7}{16}''$.
Collection V. W. van Gogh, Stedelijk Museum, Amsterdam

195. Vincent van Gogh, Peasant from the Camargue. Arles, 1888; pen-and-brush drawing; $19\frac{5}{16}'' \times 14\frac{15}{16}''$. The Fogg Museum of Art, Cambridge, Mass.

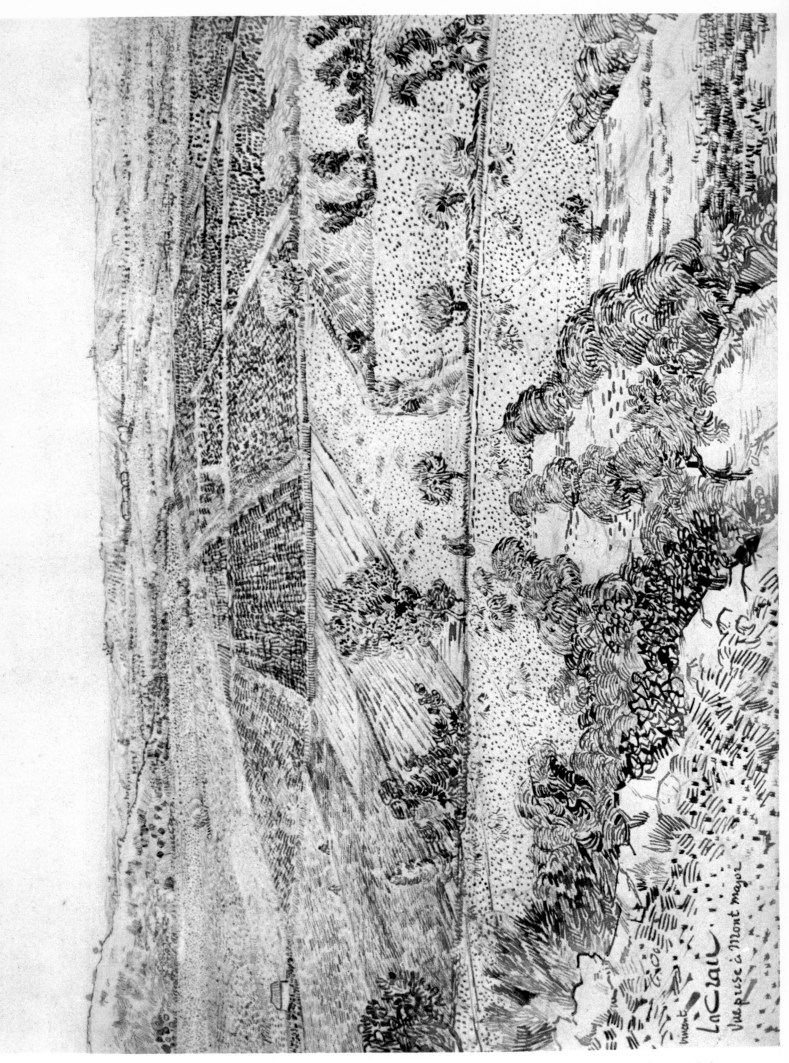

196. Vincent van Gogh, La Crau. Arles, 1888; pen-and-chalk drawing; $18\frac{7}{8}'' \times 23\frac{5}{8}''$. Collection V. W. van Gogh, Stedelijk Museum, Amsterdam

197. Vincent van Gogh, The Rock. Arles, 1888; reed pen; $19\frac{5}{16}'' \times 24''$. Collection V. W. van Gogh, Stedelijk Museum, Amsterdam

198. Vincent van Gogh, Saint-Rémy under a Starry Sky. Pen-and-brush drawing; $18\frac{1}{2}'' \times 24\frac{5}{8}''$. Formerly Kunsthalle, Bremen

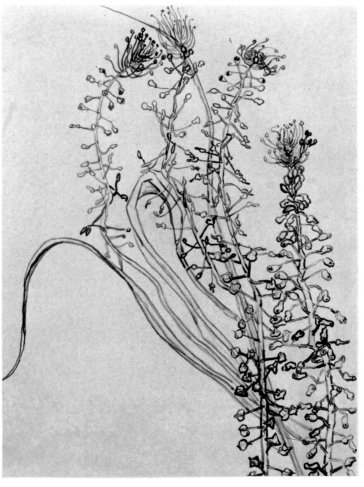

199. Vincent van Gogh, Plumed Hyacinth. Saint-Rémy, 1890; reed pen-and-pencil drawing; $16\frac{1}{8}'' \times 12\frac{3}{16}''$.
Collection V. W. van Gogh, Stedelijk Museum, Amsterdam

200. Vincent van Gogh, Peasants at Their Meal. Chalk-and-pencil drawing; $13\frac{3}{8}'' \times 19\frac{11}{16}''$. Collection V. W. van Gogh, Stedelijk Museum, Amsterdam

201. Vincent van Gogh, Town Hall, Auvers. 1890; chalk drawing; $9\frac{7}{16}'' \times 12\frac{3}{16}''$. Collection V. W. van Gogh, Stedelijk Museum, Amsterdam

202. Antoon Derkinderen, Portrait of Chaplain C. J. Tholenaer. Pencil drawing; 19$\frac{11}{16}$″ × 12$\frac{5}{8}$″. Begijnhof, Amsterdam

203. Hendrik Haverman, Portrait of Dr. J. H. C. Kern. 1896; chalk drawing; 13⁷⁄₁₆″ × 10¹⁵⁄₁₆″. Gemeente museum, The Hague

204. Willem Witsen, Portrait of Jacobus van Looy. 1891; chalk drawing; 11¾″ × 8¹¹⁄₁₆″. Witsenhuis, Amsterdam

205. Jan Veth, Portrait of Dr. Abraham Kuyper. 1892; chalk drawing; 8¹¹⁄₁₆″ × 11″. Collection F. Hinloopen, Amsterdam (1927)

206. Jan Toorop, Garden of Sorrows. 1891; chalk drawing. Collection Van Eelde, Utrecht (before 1911)

207. Jan Toorop, "O Grave, Where Is Thy Victory?" 1892; chalk drawing; $23\frac{3}{4}'' \times 29\frac{5}{8}''$. Collection W. J. R. Dreesmann, Amsterdam

208. Jan Toorop, The Apostles Thomas and Thaddeus. 1909; chalk drawing; $36\frac{7}{16}'' \times 37\frac{3}{16}''$. Stedelijk Museum, Amsterdam

209. Richard N. Roland Holst, Preaching in the Fields. 1892; chalk drawing; $22\frac{15}{16}'' \times 31\frac{1}{4}''$. Rijksprentenkabinet, Amsterdam

210. Floris Verster, Endegeest. 1893; wax crayon and water color; $16\frac{15}{16}'' \times 26\frac{3}{8}''$. Rijksmuseum Kröller-Müller, Otterlo

211. Theodoor van Hoytema, Spoonbills in a Wood. Lithograph; $12\frac{1}{16}'' \times 8\frac{1}{8}''$. Gemeentemuseum, The Hague

212. Willem Tholen, Vats in a Paper Mill at Vaassen. Chalk and water color; $14\frac{15}{16}'' \times 23\frac{7}{16}''$. Museum Boymans, Rotterdam

213. Pieter Dupont, Bank of the Seine at Paris. 1908; chalk drawing; $15\frac{3}{8}'' \times 24\frac{1}{4}''$. Rijksprentenkabinet, Amsterdam

214. Johan Thorn Prikker, Les Xhorres. 1901; chalk drawing; $22\frac{7}{16}'' \times 18\frac{1}{2}''$. Rijksmuseum Kröller-Müller, Otterlo

215. Kees van Dongen, Zandstraat, Rotterdam. Chalk and water color; 11″×17⅝″. Museum Boymans, Rotterdam

216. Kees van Dongen, The Meuse at Schiedam. Chalk drawing; 13⅝″×21⅛″. Museum Boymans, Rotterdam

217. Bart van der Leck, Street Scene. 1906; colored chalk drawing; $11\frac{7}{16}'' \times 18\frac{3}{16}''$. Rijksmuseum Kröller-Müller, Otterlo

218. Jan Sluyters, Young Woman. Chalk-and-brush drawing; $14\frac{1}{4}'' \times 10\frac{1}{2}''$. Rijksprentenkabinet, Amsterdam

219. Jan Sluyters, Couple Dancing. Chalk-and-brush drawing; $9\frac{1}{2}'' \times 6\frac{3}{4}''$. Coll. C. P. Baron van der Feltz, Amsterdam

220. Lodewijk Schelfhout, Les Angles. 1911; pen-and-brush drawing; $11\frac{13}{16}'' \times 18\frac{13}{16}''$. Gemeentemuseum, The Hague

221. Leo Gestel, Sailboats, Majorca. 1914; chalk drawing; $3\frac{3}{8}'' \times 4\frac{1}{2}''$. Rijksmuseum Kröller-Müller, Otterlo

222. Piet Mondrian, Study of a Tree. Chalk drawing; $12\frac{5}{8}'' \times 19\frac{5}{16}''$. Collection M. J. Heybroek, Hilversum

223. Piet Mondrian, Study of a Nude. 1912; charcoal; $36\frac{3}{16}'' \times 62\frac{3}{16}''$. Collection Harry Holtzman, New York

224. Piet Mondrian, Façade of the Church at Domburg. 1914; charcoal; $31\frac{1}{2}'' \times 18\frac{3}{4}''$. Collection Harry Holtzman, New York